George W. Knight

# 1-MINUTE Bible GUIDE

180 KEY PEOPLE

*Your Key to Understanding*

## BARBOUR BOOKS
An Imprint of Barbour Publishing, Inc.

© 2019 by Barbour Publishing, Inc.

Print ISBN 978-1-64352-149-7

eBook Editions:
Adobe Digital Edition (.epub) 978-1-64352-371-2
Kindle and MobiPocket Edition (.prc) 978-1-64352-372-9

All scripture quotations, unless otherwise noted, are taken from the King James Version of the Bible.

Scripture quotations marked NIV are taken from the HOLY BIBLE, NEW INTERNATIONAL VERSION®. NIV®. Copyright © 1973, 1978, 1984, 2011 by Biblica, Inc.™ Used by permission. All rights reserved worldwide.

Scripture quotations marked HCSB are taken from the Holman Christian Standard Bible ® Copyright © 1999, 2000, 2002, 2003, 2009 by Holman Bible Publishers, Nashville, Tennessee. All rights reserved.

Scripture quotations marked NLT are taken from the *Holy Bible*. New Living Translation copyright© 1996, 2004, 2015 by Tyndale House Foundation. Used by permission of Tyndale House Publishers, Inc. Carol Stream, Illinois 60188. All rights reserved.

Published by Barbour Books, an imprint of Barbour Publishing, Inc., 1810 Barbour Drive, Uhrichsville, Ohio 44683, www.barbourbooks.com

*Our mission is to inspire the world with the life-changing message of the Bible.*

Member of the
Evangelical Christian
Publishers Association

Printed in the United States of America.

# CONTENTS

## Better biblical understanding—
## in about one minute per entry.

Everyone could use a better grasp of scripture—
and the 1-Minute Bible Guide series offers you
just that. This easy-to-read book covers the 180
most important people of God's Word, offering
a representative verse and a concise description
that can be read and digested in 60 seconds or
less. And, if you want to dig deeper, most entries
include additional references for further study.

Over the course of these entries—read straight
through or one per day like a devotional—you'll
gain a clearer view of who's who in the Bible,
and why they're all important. Get better biblical
understanding—in about one minute per entry.

# AARON

*And Aaron spake all the words which
the Lord had spoken unto Moses, and did
the signs in the sight of the people.*
Exodus 4:30

The Lord chose Aaron as spokesman for Moses during the exodus from Egypt. But Aaron did more than just speak for his brother. Through God's power, he also stretched out his staff to bring one of the ten plagues against the land (Exodus 7:9, 19). In the wilderness, Aaron and Hur helped Moses hold up his hands to bring victory over the forces of Amalek (Exodus 17:12).

But Aaron also had his moments of weakness. While Moses was receiving the Ten Commandments on Mount Sinai, Aaron allowed the people to fashion an idol as an object of worship. Only Moses' intercession on his brother's behalf saved him from God's punishment (Exodus 32:3–10; Deuteronomy 9:20).

When the official priesthood was established in the wilderness, Aaron was set apart as the first high priest of Israel (Exodus 28–29). Upon his death, Aaron's son Eleazar succeeded him in this role. But this human priestly system is inferior to the priesthood of Christ. Jesus' intercession on our behalf never ends, and it offers the promise of eternal life to all believers (Hebrews 5:2–5; 7:11–12).

**Learn More:** Exodus 7:8–20 / Numbers 20:12, 29

# ABEL

*And Abel, he also brought of the firstlings of
his flock and of the fat thereof. And the Lord
had respect unto Abel and to his offering.*

GENESIS 4:4

Abel was the second son of Adam and Eve, a man whose
gift of choice animals from his flock was accepted by the
Lord (Genesis 4:1–16). He serves as a good example of
sacrificial giving.

Abel's brother Cain brought an offering of harvested
fruit and grain to the Lord, but God refused to accept it.
This made Cain angry and envious, and he murdered Abel
in the first recorded instance of violence in the Bible.

This event is mentioned several times in the New
Testament. The writer of Hebrews declared that Abel offered
a better sacrifice than his brother. This apparently refers to
Abel's faith, his superior character as a righteous person,
and the correct motives behind his gift (Hebrews 11:4). The
apostle John wrote that Cain murdered Abel because Cain's
works were evil, in comparison to the righteous acts of his
brother (1 John 3:12).

Jesus spoke of "the blood of righteous Abel" (Matthew
23:35). As the first martyr in the Bible, Abel's shed blood
symbolizes God's demand for punishment against sin
and unrighteousness. But the blood shed under the new
covenant—Jesus' atoning death on the cross—"speaketh
better things than that of Abel" (Hebrews 12:24) because it
is the agent of salvation for hopeless sinners. See also *Cain*.

**Learn More:** Genesis 4:1–25

# ABIATHAR

*And one of the sons of Ahimelech the
son of Ahitub, named Abiathar, escaped,
and fled after David.*
1 SAMUEL 22:20

Abiathar, a priest, was the sole survivor of King Saul's massacre of eighty-five priests in the city of Nob. Saul was enraged because Abiathar's father, the high priest of Nob, came to David's aid while Saul was trying to kill the future king (1 Samuel 22:6–23).

After Abiathar escaped, he lived under David's protection during David's fugitive years. When David became the unchallenged king of Israel, Abiathar emerged as a priest in the royal court (1 Samuel 30:7).

At David's orders Abiathar and another priest named Zadok took care of the ark of the covenant in Jerusalem when David fled the city to escape Absalom's rebellion. These two priests remained in Jerusalem as spies to keep the king informed of Absalom's actions (2 Samuel 15:23–29).

Abiathar had another brush with death after David passed from the scene. The priest threw his support behind the king's son Adonijah as successor to the throne. But another son, Solomon, won the power struggle. This was bad news for any subject who was not totally loyal to the new regime, and Solomon promptly banished Abiathar and his family from Jerusalem. Only his previous loyalty to David saved the priest from execution (1 Kings 2:26–27).

**Learn More:** 2 Samuel 19:11–15

# ABIGAIL

*And David said to Abigail, Blessed be
the L*ORD *God of Israel, which sent
thee this day to meet me.*
1 SAMUEL 25:32

Abigail's quick thinking and sound advice kept David from making a terrible mistake. It all started when David was on the run from Saul in Abigail's territory. He asked her husband, Nabal, to provide food for his hungry men. Nabal refused and insulted David by calling him a no-good leader of a band of outlaws.

When Abigail learned about this, she gathered the provisions David had asked for and set off toward his camp. She met a man boiling with anger—David had his men armed and ready to settle the score with Abigail's husband.

But she urged David not to return one foolish act with another, reminding David that he was destined to become the next king of Israel. Surely he didn't want a thoughtless act of revenge as a blot on his record. David saw the wisdom in Abigail's reasoning and had his men stand down (1 Samuel 25:1–35).

Several days after Abigail returned home, Nabal died following a drunken orgy. When David heard the news, he took Abigail as his wife. She became the mother of one of David's sons (2 Samuel 3:3).

**Learn More:** 1 Chronicles 3:1–9

# ABNER

*And David said. . .mourn before Abner.*
*And king David himself followed the bier.*
2 SAMUEL 3:31

Abner was a chief military officer under both King Saul and King David. Abner was on the scene when David the shepherd boy defeated the Philistine giant Goliath. When Saul asked about the boy, Abner looked David up and introduced him to the king. Abner led Saul's army during the years when David hid from Saul in the wilderness.

After Saul was killed in a battle with the Philistines, a power struggle broke out between David's supporters and those who favored Ish-bosheth, one of Saul's sons. Abner threw his support behind Ish-bosheth.

Later, Abner changed his mind, shifted his loyalty to David, and convinced other influential leaders to do the same. But just as things were going David's way, he faced another crisis. Joab, commander of David's army, murdered Abner to avenge Abner's killing of Joab's brother.

David realized this would look like an assassination he had plotted. This could undermine the support of Abner's friends. So the king reprimanded Joab publicly and arranged for Abner to be buried with full honors.

**Learn More:** 1 Samuel 17:55–58; 26:14–15 / 2 Samuel 3:17–38

# ABRAHAM

*Now the L&#42;ORD had said unto Abram,*
*Get thee out of thy country, and from thy*
*kindred, and from thy father's house,*
*unto a land that I will shew thee.*
GENESIS 12:1

God's determination to build a special people who would be devoted to Him began with Abraham. The Lord called him to leave his native land for a place that would be revealed to him in due time. Abraham obeyed and moved into Canaan, a land that God promised to give to him and his descendants (Genesis 12:1–5).

The problem was that Abraham had no children, and the prospects of having any were bleak because of his advanced age. The Lord solved this dilemma by allowing his wife Sarah to conceive and give birth to Isaac in their old age (Genesis 21:1–8). Abraham had fathered a previous son through Sarah's servant. But God made it clear that His promise to Abraham was to be fulfilled through Isaac (Genesis 17:20–21).

To test Abraham's faith, the Lord directed him to sacrifice his beloved son Isaac. Then God himself stepped in to save the boy and renewed His promise to bless Abraham because of his great faith (Genesis 22:1–12). Abraham lived to the age of 175 and was buried beside Sarah in a cave he had purchased near the city of Hebron (Genesis 25:7–10).

**Learn More:** Genesis 20:1–17; 25:1–6 / Psalm 105:6–10 / Romans 4:1–3 / Matthew 1:1–2

# ABSALOM

*And the king said, Let him turn to his*
*own house, and let him not see my face.*
*So Absalom returned to his own house,*
*and saw not the king's face.*
2 SAMUEL 14:24

When David committed adultery with Bathsheba, the prophet Nathan predicted that his family would be struck with tragedy because of this sin (2 Samuel 12:9–12). A chain of family difficulties finally reached its climax when David's own son, Absalom, tried to take the kingship by force.

This all began with another tragedy. Absalom ordered the murder of his half brother Amnon for molesting their sister Tamar (2 Samuel 13:22–32). Absalom then fled from Jerusalem. Although David loved Absalom dearly, he refused to communicate with him, even after he returned to the city. This shunning may have been one reason why Absalom tried to take down his father (2 Samuel 14:24–28).

During a battle with David's forces, Absalom's long hair got entangled in the branch of a tree. He was killed by Joab, David's commander (2 Samuel 18:9–14).

When David heard the news, he wept with some of the saddest words in the Bible. "O my son Absalom! My son, my son Absalom!" he cried. "If only I had died instead of you—O Absalom, my son, my son!" (2 Samuel 18:33 NIV).

**Learn More:** 2 Samuel 15:1–12

# ACHAN

*And Achan answered Joshua, and said,*
*Indeed I have sinned against the L*ord *God of*
*Israel, and thus and thus have I done.*
Joshua 7:20

Before Joshua led an attack on the city of Jericho, God made it clear that no one was to claim the spoils of war for himself. These were to be consecrated to God and placed in "the treasury of the Lord" (Joshua 6:19).

But an Israelite soldier named Achan took several valuable articles from the booty and hid them in his tent. Meanwhile, the Israelites attacked the small town of Ai. Compared to Jericho, Ai should have been an easy target, since it had only a few defenders. But surprisingly, the Israelites suffered a humiliating defeat.

Joshua prayed for an answer to the dilemma, and the Lord revealed that someone had disobeyed His command. A thorough search brought Achan's forbidden cache to light. He had taken a Babylonian garment, two hundred shekels of silver, and a wedge of gold.

Achan and his family were taken to a nearby valley, where they were stoned to death (Joshua 7:1–26). Soon thereafter, the Israelites attacked Ai again and won an easy victory (Joshua 8:21–26).

**Learn More:** 1 Chronicles 2:7; *Achar:* KJV / Joshua 22:20

# ADAM

*And the* LORD *God formed man of the dust of the ground, and breathed into his nostrils the breath of life.*

GENESIS 2:7

Adam was the crowning achievement of the creation (Genesis 1:26). But he was fashioned from the dust of the ground, symbolizing his humble status as an earthbound being who owed his existence to the Lord.

God placed Adam in the garden of Eden and gave him the task of working the ground (Genesis 2:15). The fruit from all the trees in the garden were his for the taking—with one exception. He was not to eat from the tree of the knowledge of good and evil (Genesis 2:17).

Eve, Adam's female counterpart, yielded to temptation from Satan and ate the forbidden fruit, then encouraged Adam to do the same. This act of disobedience led God to banish the couple from the garden and to subject them to a life of difficulties (Genesis 3:1–24).

Adam's rebellion against God was the original transgression that infected the entire human race (Romans 3:23). But according to the apostle Paul, God sent another Adam—the Last Adam, Jesus Christ—to solve the problem caused by the original man. Adam's legacy of death has been canceled by the atoning death of Jesus on the cross (1 Corinthians 15:21–22). See also *Eve*.

**Learn More:** Luke 3:38

# ADONIJAH

*Then Adonijah the son of Haggith exalted himself, saying, I will be king: and he prepared him chariots and horsemen, and fifty men to run before him.*
1 Kings 1:5

Adonijah was a son of King David whose ambition got him into trouble. While his father was still alive, he made a bold move to set himself up as David's successor.

When the king was old and in failing health, Adonijah summoned his supporters, including several of David's other sons, to a meeting near Jerusalem. David's son Solomon was not invited (1 Kings 1:18–19), so Adonijah must have known that Solomon was the king's choice as his successor.

But several people, including Solomon's mother, Bathsheba, hurried to the king to tell him what was going on. They convinced David to have Solomon anointed immediately as the new king.

When Adonijah heard the news, he realized his kingly ambitions were over, and even worse, that Solomon could kill him. He fled to the tabernacle and grabbed the horns of the altar, an act that supposedly guaranteed his safety. Solomon released him with a warning not to cause any more trouble (1 Kings 1:50–52).

Later, Adonijah asked Solomon to let him marry Abishag, the young woman who had served as David's nurse in his old age. Solomon apparently interpreted this as evidence that he still had kingly ambitions, so he had Adonijah executed (1 Kings 2:13–25).

**Learn More:** 1 Chronicles 3:1–2

# AGRIPPA

*Then Agrippa said unto Paul, Thou art permitted
to speak for thyself. Then Paul stretched forth
the hand, and answered for himself.*

ACTS 26:1

Agrippa was a Roman official before whom the apostle Paul
appeared while imprisoned at Caesarea. The apostle made a
passionate speech in which he recounted the events of his
life, particularly his conversion from persecutor to preacher
of the Christian faith (Acts 26:1–27).

Paul ended his speech with a direct appeal to Agrippa to
believe the prophecies about Jesus, whom God had raised
from the dead. "King Agrippa, do you believe the prophets?"
he asked. "I know you do" (verse 27 NIV).

Agrippa responded, "Almost thou persuadest me to be
a Christian" (verse 28). Was he on the verge of becoming
a believer, or was he being sarcastic? It's impossible to say
for sure. One modern translation renders his response
like this: "Do you think you can persuade me to become a
Christian so quickly?" (NLT).

Either way, Agrippa was impressed with Paul's stirring
defense. He declared that the apostle was innocent and
could be set free had he not appealed his case to Rome
(Acts 26:32).

This Agrippa is often referred to as Agrippa II, to
distinguish him from his father, Agrippa I, who persecuted
the Christians in Jerusalem (Acts 12:1–23).

**Learn More:** Acts 25:13–27

# AHAB

*And Ahab the son of Omri did evil in the sight*
*of the Lord above all that were before him.*
1 Kings 16:30

Ahab had a lot going for him when he took the throne of the northern kingdom of Israel. His father had built a new capital city, and the country was in good shape financially. Ahab built several new cities throughout the nation (1 Kings 22:39) and established peaceful relations with Judah, the sister nation to the south (1 Kings 22:2–4).

Ahab's problems began with his political marriage to Jezebel, daughter of a Phoenician king. She worshipped the pagan god Baal, and she influenced Ahab to allow Baal worship throughout the nation. The king even built a temple to Baal in the capital city (1 Kings 16:32–33).

Ahab's greed also got him into trouble. He wanted a plot of ground near his summer palace. But the landowner, Naboth, refused to sell. With Jezebel's help, the two had Naboth executed on a false charge of blasphemy. Then the king confiscated the property (1 Kings 21:1–16).

The prophet Elijah predicted that God would punish the king severely for this crime (1 Kings 21:19). Several years later Ahab was killed in a battle with the Syrians. When his blood was flushed from his chariot, dogs lapped up the bloody water (1 Kings 22:38).

**Learn More:** 1 Kings 20:1–21

# AHASUERUS

*And the king loved Esther above all the women,
and she obtained grace and favour in his sight
more than all the virgins; so that he set the
royal crown upon her head, and made
her queen instead of Vashti.*
ESTHER 2:17

A king of Persia, Ahasuerus is portrayed throughout the book of Esther as a sensual pleasure-seeker (1:7–8) who was vain (1:4), quick-tempered (1:13–22), and subject to manipulation by others (3:1–15). But he did have the good sense to select the young Jewish woman Esther as his queen.

Ahasuerus deposed his first queen, Vashti, because she refused his command to display her beauty to his drunken guests. Esther eventually succeeded Vashti in the royal court.

Some time later, the king's second-in-command—a man named Haman—convinced Ahasuerus to issue a death order against all Jewish people throughout his kingdom. This act of retaliation against an entire race came about because one Jewish man, Mordecai, refused to bow down and pay homage to Haman (Esther 3:1–11).

When Esther learned about the plot, she used her influence with the king to expose Haman, have him executed, and save her people from genocide. Ahasuerus issued a second proclamation that allowed the Jews to defend themselves against the original death order (Esther 8:11–13).

**Learn More:** Esther 6:1–10

# AMALEK

*And Joshua discomfited Amalek and
his people with the edge of the sword.*
Exodus 17:13

Amalek was a grandson of Esau, Jacob's twin brother. Amalek was the ancestor of a tribal group known as the Amalekites, fierce enemies of the Israelites. They lived in southern Canaan, the land promised by the Lord to Abraham and his descendants.

Amalek as a person is cited only three times in the Bible (Genesis 36:12, 16; 1 Chronicles 1:36). But the Amalekites as a tribe are mentioned throughout the Old Testament. In the King James Version, the singular name *Amalek* is often used to refer to this tribe, as in Exodus 17:13.

While wandering in the wilderness, the Israelites were attacked by the Amalekites. Under Joshua's leadership, the Israelites won the battle—but only because Moses held his hands up over the battle scene. Aaron and Hur steadied his hands when Moses grew tired (Exodus 17:8–13).

In later years, campaigns against the Amalekites were conducted by King Saul (1 Samuel 15:1–5) and King David (1 Samuel 27:8–10).

**Learn More:** Genesis 36:1–12

# AMAZIAH

*Now it came to pass, after that Amaziah*
*was come from the slaughter of the Edomites,*
*that he brought the gods of the children*
*of Seir, and set them up to be his gods,*
*and bowed down himself before them,*
*and burned incense unto them.*

2 Chronicles 25:14

King Amaziah of Judah got off to a good start by following the Lord. But he soon found trouble because of his flawed judgment and poor choices.

The king's problems began when he won a decisive victory over the Edomites. For some strange reason, he adopted their pagan gods as his own and began to worship them in his homeland. It was as if the Edomites lost the battle but won a war for Amaziah's heart.

God was angered by this turn of events, so He sent a prophet to ask the king a sobering question: "Why have you sought a people's gods that could not deliver their own people from your hands?" (2 Chronicles 25:15 HCSB).

Energized by his victory over Edom, Amaziah foolishly renewed hostilities against Israel, Judah's sister Jewish kingdom to the north. This time he suffered a humiliating defeat. The Israelite army attacked Jerusalem and carried away captives as well as treasures from the temple and Amaziah's palace (2 Chronicles 25:20–24).

**Learn More:** 2 Kings 14:1–6, 17–19

# AMNON

*And Amnon was so vexed, that he fell sick
for his sister Tamar; for she was a virgin;
and Amnon thought it hard for
him to do anything to her.*

2 SAMUEL 13:2

Just like his father David before him, Amnon's sexual desires caused a chain reaction of family tragedies. He was so infatuated with his half-sister Tamar that he forced himself upon her (2 Samuel 13:1–20). This caused her great shame and humiliation. It also led Absalom, Tamar's full brother, to avenge this crime by murdering Amnon (2 Samuel 13:22–29).

Another spin-off of this tragic event was the alienation of Absalom from his father, David. The king treated Absalom as an outcast and apparently did not speak to him for several years (2 Samuel 14:24, 28, 33). This ill will between father and son eventually led Absalom to rebel against David's authority and to try to take the throne by force (2 Samuel 15:1–14).

If not for Amnon's sin that led to his death, he could have been in line to succeed David as king. He was his father's oldest son, born while David ruled southern Judah from the city of Hebron (2 Samuel 3:2).

**Learn More:** 2 Samuel 13:30–33

# AMOS

*The words of Amos. . .which he saw concerning
Israel in the days of Uzziah king of Judah, and in
the days of Jeroboam the son of Joash king of
Israel, two years before the earthquake.*
AMOS 1:1

The prophet Amos admitted he was simply a shepherd
and a farmer. But God called him to deliver a message of
judgment against the northern kingdom of Israel. This was
all the authority he needed to speak on behalf of the Lord
(Amos 7:15–16). His prophecies appear in the Old Testament
book that bears his name.

The prophet condemned the people of Israel because
they had rejected the Lord and turned to the worship of
false gods. He also criticized the wealthy class for oppressing
the poor (Amos 2:6).

Amos insisted that righteous behavior—not observing
empty rituals such as feast days and bringing sacrifices to
the altar—was what God required of His people. "Let justice
roll on like a river," he declared, "righteousness like a never-
failing stream" (Amos 5:24 NIV).

The prophet is well known for the visions he received
from the Lord. One of the most striking was a basket of
ripe fruit. Like these delicacies that would quickly spoil in
the summer heat, Israel was overdue for God's judgment
because of her disobedience of the Lord (Amos 8:1–2).

**Learn More:** Amos 7:7–9

# ANANIAS

*Then Ananias answered, Lord, I have heard
by many of this man, how much evil he
hath done to thy saints at Jerusalem.*
ACTS 9:13

Ananias, a believer in the city of Damascus, could have been persecuted by the man who became the apostle Paul. Instead, Ananias was the instrument God used to help Paul and commission him as a preacher of the Gospel (Acts 9:10–20).

The apostle, then known as Saul, was headed to Damascus to persecute its Christians when he was gloriously converted. In the process, he was struck blind for three days, and the Lord called Ananias to put his hands on Paul so his sight could be restored.

Because of Paul's reputation as a fierce enemy of the church, Ananias was reluctant to obey God. But he did after the Lord explained that Paul had been selected as His special witness who would lead many people, including Gentiles, to the Lord.

This Ananias is the second of three men by that name in the book of Acts. The first mentioned was struck dead for lying about the amount of money he had given to the Lord's work (Acts 5:1–11). The third is the high priest in Jerusalem, who was involved in Paul's trial (Acts 23:1–5).

**Learn More:** Acts 22:11–16

# ANDREW

*He [Andrew] first findeth his own brother Simon,
and saith unto him, We have found the Messias,
which is, being interpreted, the Christ.*
JOHN 1:41

After becoming one of Jesus' disciples, Andrew always seemed to be introducing other people to the Lord. At first, Andrew was a follower of John the Baptist, but he turned to Jesus after John identified Him as "the Lamb of God." Andrew spent a day at Jesus' home, then went immediately to his brother Peter to introduce him to the Master (John 1:37–42).

Later, Andrew told Jesus about a boy who had brought his lunch to an isolated place where many people had gathered. Jesus multiplied the boy's loaves and fish to feed the hungry crowd (John 6:1–11). This event became known as the miracle of the feeding of the five thousand.

On another occasion, Andrew and Philip—another member of the Twelve—told Jesus about a group of Greeks who wanted to talk with Him (John 12:20–22). Andrew is mentioned a final time in the Gospels when he asked Jesus about the events of the end times (Mark 13:3–4).

**Learn More:** Acts 1:8–14

# ANNA

*And she [Anna] coming in that instant
gave thanks likewise unto the Lord,
and spake of him to all them that
looked for redemption in Jerusalem.*
LUKE 2:38

Jewish custom dictated that all firstborn sons be presented, along with an offering, at the temple in Jerusalem. Mary and Joseph observed this custom when Jesus was eight days old (Luke 2:22–38).

In the building that day was an aged widow named Anna. A prophetess, she was probably a temple attendant, since she "departed not from the temple, but served God with fastings and prayers night and day" (Luke 2:37).

Through divine revelation, Anna recognized this eight-day-old boy as the long-awaited Messiah. She broke out in praise to the Lord for sending Jesus as the agent of redemption for His people.

Anna is a good example of how to grow old gracefully. She remained faithful to the Lord in spite of the loss of her husband at a young age. She communed constantly with her Lord through prayer. And she never lost faith that God would fulfill His promise.

# APOLLOS

*For he [Apollos] mightily convinced the
Jews, and that publicly, shewing by the
scriptures that Jesus was Christ.*
ACTS 18:28

Some time after the apostle Paul founded the church at
Ephesus, a zealous and learned believer named Apollos
visited the city. He used his knowledge of the Old Testament
scriptures to convince the Jews in the local synagogue that
Jesus was the Messiah they had been looking for (Acts
18:24–28).

Aquila and Priscilla, two leaders in the church at Ephesus,
heard about his powerful preaching. Apollos had been
a disciple of John the Baptist, so apparently he had an
inadequate understanding of the gospel message. These
two leaders befriended Apollos and "explained the way of
God even more accurately" (verse 26 NLT).

Apollos went on to become a popular preacher,
particularly in Achaia (verse 27) and the church at Corinth.
A faction of Corinthian believers favored Apollos over
all other human leaders. Paul dealt with this problem by
pointing out that Jesus was the true source and foundation of their faith (1 Corinthians 3:3–11).

Apollos may also have served on the island of Crete.
Paul encouraged Titus, leader of this church, to send two
believers—one of whom was named Apollos—on their way
with everything they needed for the journey (Titus 3:13).

**Learn More:** 1 Corinthians 4:1–7

# ASA

*And Asa did that which was right in the eyes
of the LORD, as did David his father.*

1 KINGS 15:11

Asa, the third king of Judah, presided over many religious reforms in the land. He removed the idols that had been erected during the reign of Abijam, his father and predecessor. He restored the altar in the temple and encouraged the people to renew their covenant with the Lord. He even deposed his own mother from power because she had set up a shrine devoted to a pagan god (1 Kings 15:9–13).

But the king's record was not perfect. After winning a victory over the Ethiopians by relying on the Lord, he hired an army from Syria to turn back an assault by Israel, Judah's sister kingdom to the north. A prophet named Hanani rebuked Asa for relying on foreign soldiers rather than trusting the Lord. Enraged, the king had the prophet thrown into prison (2 Chronicles 16:1–10).

Before his reign ended, Asa developed a foot disease. The recorder of his administration noted that "he did not seek help from the LORD, but only from the physicians" (2 Chronicles 16:12 NIV). Asa is mentioned in the New Testament, in Matthew's genealogy of Jesus (Matthew 1:7).

**Learn More:** 2 Chronicles 14:1–15; 15:1–16; 16:1–14

# ASAPH

*So the singers, Heman, Asaph, and Ethan, were*
*appointed to sound with cymbals of brass.*
1 CHRONICLES 15:19

A Levite musician in David's time, Asaph was responsible for sounding cymbals in praise to the Lord when the ark of the covenant was relocated to Jerusalem. This was a joyous occasion for all the people of the city. They joined in the celebration with "shouting, and with sound of the cornet, and with trumpets, and with cymbals, making a noise with psalteries and with harps" (1 Chronicles 15:28). King David himself was so excited that he danced before the ark as it entered the city.

In later years, David organized the priests and Levites of Judah into units and assigned them specific responsibilities to perform. Asaph and his descendants were charged with providing music for worship at the tabernacle. Their work as musicians carried over to the temple after it was built under King Solomon (1 Chronicles 25:1–9).

After the exile, descendants of Asaph returned to Jerusalem and led the singing at the dedication of the foundation of the rebuilt temple (Ezra 2:41; 3:10–11). Twelve psalms (Psalms 50; 73–83) are identified as "psalms of Asaph" or given similar titles.

**Learn More:** Psalm 73

# ATHALIAH

*And when Athaliah the mother of Ahaziah*
*saw that her son was dead, she arose*
*and destroyed all the seed royal.*
2 KINGS 11:1

Athaliah grew up in a political family as the daughter of a king of Israel (2 Kings 8:26). So she was ready to make a political move of her own during the chaos that followed the assassination of her son, King Ahaziah of Judah. She promptly executed her own grandsons to eliminate any possible claimants to the throne and took control as queen of Judah.

But the Lord saw to it that the ruthless queen missed one grandson, Joash, who was only a year old at the time. For six years the young prince was hidden in the temple. Then Jehoiada, the high priest, brought the boy out of hiding. The priest rallied the people to execute Athaliah and replace her with Joash as the rightful claimant to the throne (2 Kings 11:1–20).

Athaliah was the only woman and the only non-descendant of David to occupy the throne of Judah. But thanks to Jehoiada and others, she did not destroy the royal Davidic line from which the Messiah eventually emerged.

**Learn More:** 2 Chronicles 22:10–23:21

# AUGUSTUS

*And it came to pass in those days, that there
went out a decree from Caesar Augustus
that all the world should be taxed.*

LUKE 2:1

*Augustus* was a title of honor, meaning "his reverence,"
that was bestowed on all emperors of the Roman Empire
after his death (see, for example, Acts 25:21). This first
Augustus issued the census decree for taxation purposes
that brought Mary and Joseph to Bethlehem, where Jesus
was born. Augustus's policies, including taxation of all
subject nations, led to the extension of the boundaries of
the empire and the development of its capital city, Rome.

Augustus has been identified by secular historians as
Octavian (ruled 31 BC–AD 14). Thus he was alive during
Jesus' boyhood years, before the Lord launched His public
ministry.

# BALAAM

*How shall I [Balaam] curse, whom God*
*hath not cursed? or how shall I defy,*
*whom the LORD hath not defied?*
NUMBERS 23:8

Balaam, a pagan wizard, shows that God can use even an evil force to bring about His will.

The king of Moab had hired Balaam to pronounce a curse against the Israelites as they passed through his territory on their way to Canaan. But God intervened and caused Balaam to bless the Israelites instead. This happened not once but three times (Numbers 24:1–11).

Enraged at this turn of events, the king refused to pay the generous fee he had promised for Balaam's services. Then the wizard predicted, "A star will come from Jacob, and a scepter will arise from Israel" (Numbers 24:17 HCSB). This has been interpreted as a reference to Jesus the Messiah.

Balaam is best known as the man with a talking donkey. When he set out to find the Israelite camp, his donkey balked because the angel of the Lord blocked their path. The donkey detoured around the angel three times until Balaam finally beat the innocent beast with a stick. At this the donkey told his master, "What have I done unto thee, that thou hast smitten me these three times?" (Numbers 22:28).

The moral of the story is probably Balaam's lack of spiritual sensitivity. A simple donkey saw the angel of the Lord, while Balaam—supposed to have magical powers—was blind to what God was doing.

**Learn More:** Numbers 23–24 / Joshua 13:22 / Jude 11 / 2 Peter 2:15 / Revelation 2:14

# BARABBAS

*And they cried out all at once, saying, Away*
*with this man, and release unto us Barabbas.*
LUKE 23:18

Locked away in prison on the day of Jesus' crucifixion was a notorious criminal named Barabbas. Pilate asked the crowd whether they wanted him or Jesus released from custody. The crowd, agitated by the religious leaders, chose Barabbas.

During the Passover celebration that was going on at the time, Roman authorities apparently released one prisoner as a goodwill gesture to the Jewish people. Barabbas had led a revolt against the authority of Rome. The people hated their Roman overlords, so they naturally clamored for Barabbas rather than Jesus to be set free (Matthew 27:15–22).

The contrast between this criminal and Jesus could not be more dramatic. One was a military leader, the other a spiritual Savior. One called for political deliverance from the power of Rome; the other offered hope for spiritual deliverance from the darkness of sin.

**Learn More:** Mark 15:6–15 / John 18:39–40

# BARNABAS

*But Barnabas took him [Paul], and*
*brought him to the apostles, and*
*declared. . .how he had preached boldly*
*at Damascus in the name of Jesus.*
ACTS 9:27

The name of Barnabas, a believer in the early church, means "son of encouragement." He lived up to his name by speaking up for Paul when many Christians did not trust the former persecutor of the church (Acts 9:27–28).

After Barnabas became a leader in the church at Antioch, he enlisted Paul to help him in this ministry (Acts 11:19–26). Later, the church sent Barnabas and Paul to witness in territories that had not been reached by the gospel. Barnabas was in the lead when they left, but Paul had moved to the forefront by the time they returned. This trip eventually became known as the apostle's first missionary journey (Acts 13:1–3; 14:26–28).

Barnabas would have been with Paul on his second journey, if not for a disagreement between them. Barnabas wanted to take his relative John Mark with them as he had done before. But Paul refused because the young man had returned home without completing the first missionary tour. So Barnabas left Paul, took Mark with him, and set off in a different direction (Acts 15:36–41).

**Learn More:** Acts 4:36–37; 11:29–30; 12:25; 15:1–2

# BARTIMAEUS

*And when he [Bartimaeus] heard that it was
Jesus of Nazareth, he began to cry out, and say,
Jesus, thou son of David, have mercy on me.*
MARK 10:47

Bartimaeus, a blind beggar from the city of Jericho, is a study in perseverance. He was sitting by the road begging for handouts when Jesus passed by. He had heard about this miraculous teacher and healer, so he called out above the noise of the crowd for Jesus to make him well.

Some people standing nearby told Bartimaeus to stop yelling, but he shouted even louder to get Jesus' attention (Mark 10:46–52).

Jesus heard the blind man, called him over, and asked him what he wanted. Then the Lord restored the man's sight with the words, "Go thy way; thy faith hath made thee whole" (verse 52). Bartimaeus's faith and determination were richly rewarded.

Accounts of the healing of a blind man at Jericho also appear in the gospels of Matthew and Luke, but only Mark identifies him as Bartimaeus.

**Learn More:** Matthew 20:29–34 / Luke 18:35–43

# BATHSHEBA

*Even as I [David] sware unto thee by the L*ORD
*God of Israel, saying, Assuredly Solomon thy
[Bathsheba's] son shall reign after me.*
1 KINGS 1:30

Bathsheba was a mother who wanted the best for her son. As a wife of King David and the mother of Solomon, she used her influence with the king to ensure that her son would follow David on the throne.

Bathsheba became David's wife after their adulterous affair resulted in the birth of a son. This child died as an infant. Later, she gave birth to Solomon, one of four children she bore to David (2 Samuel 12:24; 1 Chronicles 3:5).

David had many sons by several different wives (1 Chronicles 3:1–9), so it was not surprising that a dispute erupted over which one would be his successor. The fourth-born, Adonijah, enlisted supporters and declared himself the legitimate successor to the throne. This brought Bathsheba and Nathan the prophet on the run to confront David.

These two insisted that David declare publicly that he wanted Solomon to succeed him. The king not only agreed, but he made arrangements for Solomon to be sworn in immediately as the new king (1 Kings 1:15–30).

**Learn More:** 2 Samuel 11:1–27; *Bathshua:* KJV

*Then was king Belshazzar greatly troubled, and his countenance was changed in him, and his lords were astonied.*

DANIEL 5:9

Belshazzar, king of Babylon, threw a rowdy banquet for his top officials. Their revelry was interrupted when a human hand appeared and wrote a message on the wall of the royal palace: "Mene, Mene, Tekel, Upharsin." The king was so frightened by this ghostly image that "the joints of his loins were loosed, and his knees smote one against another" (Daniel 5:6; see 5:1–31).

None of Belshazzar's court magicians could tell what the writing meant. So his queen urged him to summon Daniel, a Jewish exile in Babylon who was known for his wisdom and understanding.

Daniel chastised the king for his pride and disrespect. He and his guests had been drinking from sacred vessels stolen by the Babylonians from the Jewish temple in Jerusalem. Then the prophet turned to the strange handwriting on the wall. It meant that the king had been measured by the Lord and found wanting. Belshazzar's kingdom was coming to an end; it would fall to a stronger world power.

As it turned out, Belshazzar was the last king of the mighty Babylonian Empire. That very night he was killed when his nation fell to the Persian army (Daniel 5:30–31).

**Learn More:** Daniel 7:1; 8:1

# BENJAMIN

*And it came to pass, as her [Rachel's] soul was in departing, (for she died) that she called his name Benoni: but his father called him Benjamin.*
GENESIS 35:18

Rachel had such difficulty delivering Benjamin that she gave him a name meaning "son of my pain." She died soon after he was born. But Jacob changed his son's name to one that means "son of the right hand" (Genesis 35:16–20).

The name shows that Jacob, who had children by four women, felt a special affection for this son of his favorite wife. He had displayed the same favoritism toward Joseph, Rachel's other son and Benjamin's only full brother (Genesis 43:29–34).

Joseph's jealous half brothers had sold him into slavery, but God brought him into leadership in Egypt. When all of Jacob's sons were eventually reunited, Joseph welcomed each with a kiss of affection—but he was so glad to see his full brother that he "threw his arms around Benjamin and wept, and Benjamin wept on his shoulder" (Genesis 45:14 HCSB).

Benjamin's descendants grew into the tribe of Benjamin, one of the twelve tribes of Israel. Two notable Benjamites mentioned in the Bible are Saul, the first king of Israel (1 Samuel 10:20–24), and Paul, apostle to the Gentiles (Romans 11:1).

When King Solomon's united kingdom split into two factions following his death, the tribe of Benjamin joined the tribe of Judah in remaining loyal to the house of David. They comprised the nation of Judah, also known as the southern kingdom.

**Learn More:** Genesis 46:21 / Numbers 26:38–41

# BILDAD

*Now when Job's three friends heard of all*
*this evil that was come upon him, they*
*came every one from his own place. . .*
*to mourn with him and to comfort him.*

JOB 2:11

After Job lost his family and possessions, Bildad was one of the three friends who came to offer sympathy. The other two were Elihu and Zophar. For seven days the men just sat with Job in silence. But when they began to speak, they became accusers rather than friends.

Bildad told Job that his claim to be an innocent sufferer was nothing but a "blustering wind" (Job 8:2 NIV). He was certain that Job had sinned and that this was the reason for his affliction (Job 8:5–6).

In one of his responses to Bildad's accusations, Job basically called him a know-it-all. "How you have enlightened my stupidity!" he exclaimed in a tone dripping with sarcasm. "Where have you gotten all these wise sayings?" (Job 26:3–4 NLT).

Bildad and his friends were eventually reprimanded for their misguided attempts to explain how and why the Lord was dealing with Job. Job prayed for them, and God restored Job's fortunes (Job 42:7–10). See also *Job*.

**Learn More:** Job 18; 25

# BOAZ

*Then said Boaz unto Ruth, Hearest thou
not, my daughter? Go not to glean in
another field, neither go from hence,
but abide here fast by my maidens.*
RUTH 2:8

Boaz, a wealthy landowner of Bethlehem, was kind to Ruth
when she came to his fields to glean—that is, to gather
leftover grain for herself and her mother-in-law, Naomi
(Ruth 2:1–23). Both Ruth and Naomi were destitute widows
who had to forage in the fields near Bethlehem to support
themselves.

Later, Naomi told Ruth that Boaz was a distant relative
of her late husband. At Naomi's encouragement, Ruth lay
down at Boaz's feet while he slept to signify her willingness to
marry him. Under Old Testament law, a man was encouraged
to marry the widow of his deceased relative in order to
produce children to carry on the family name.

Boaz wanted to marry Ruth, but had to reach an
agreement with another relative who was first in line. That
done, Boaz took Ruth as his wife. From their union came a
son named Obed, grandfather of the great King David of
Israel (Ruth 4:21–22).

Boaz is listed in the two genealogies of Jesus in the New
Testament (Matthew 1:5; Luke 3:32; *Booz*: KJV). See also *Ruth*.

**Learn More:** 1 Chronicles 2:11–12

# CAIAPHAS

*Then the high priest [Caiaphas] rent his
clothes, saying, He hath spoken blasphemy;
what further need have we of witnesses?
behold, now ye have heard his blasphemy.*
MATTHEW 26:65

Caiaphas was the high priest who presided over the Sanhedrin, the religious high court of the Jewish people. After Lazarus was raised from the dead, members of this body were disturbed by Jesus' growing popularity among the people. Caiaphas declared that Jesus had to die, and led the plot to have Jesus arrested (John 11:44–54).

The high priest also led the questioning of Jesus at His trial, and probably sanctioned the search for two false witnesses who testified against Jesus. Caiaphas pronounced the court's verdict of capital punishment against Jesus for violating Jewish laws against blasphemy, or assuming authority that belonged only to God (Matthew 26:57–67).

Caiaphas continued his opposition to Jesus even after the resurrection and ascension. He was one of the religious leaders who questioned Peter and John about their healing of a lame man at the temple in Jerusalem (Acts 3:1–8; 4:6–7).

The remains of a "Caiaphas," along with those of his family members, have been discovered by archaeologists in a burial cave in Jerusalem. But it is not known for certain if they belong to this opponent of Jesus.

**Learn More:** Matthew 26:3–5 / Luke 3:2

# CAIN

*And the L*ORD *said unto Cain, Where is Abel*
*thy brother? And he said, I know not:*
*Am I my brother's keeper?*
GENESIS 4:9

The oldest son of Adam and Eve, Cain will always be remembered as the man who committed the first act of violence recorded in the Bible. He murdered his brother Abel out of jealousy because Abel's offering was accepted by the Lord while his was not (Genesis 4:3–16). Cain, a farmer, offered the Lord fruits he had grown, while his brother, a shepherd, presented a sacrificial lamb from his flock.

God punished Cain by sending him into exile. Cain protested that this made him an easy target for anyone who wanted to avenge Abel's murder. So in an act of compassion, God marked Cain to keep this from happening. Cain eventually had a son, and he founded a city known as Enoch that he named for his son (Genesis 4:17).

In the New Testament, the apostle John reminded believers to love one another, unlike Cain, "who belonged to the evil one and murdered his brother" (1 John 3:12 NIV). See also *Abel*.

**Learn More:** Hebrews 11:4

# CALEB

*And Caleb stilled the people before Moses,
and said, Let us go up at once, and possess
it; for we are well able to overcome it.*
NUMBERS 13:30

While the Israelites were in the wilderness, Moses selected a scouting party to investigate the land of Canaan. Caleb was a member of this task force (Numbers 13:1–21).

The scouts returned with good news and bad news: The land was fertile and productive, but it was inhabited by fierce people who would not be easy to defeat. Ten members of the group advised against entering the land. But Caleb—along with Joshua—declared the Israelites should place their faith in the Lord and move on Canaan immediately (Numbers 14:6–9).

God punished the faithless Israelites by sentencing them to forty more years of fruitless wandering in the wilderness. During this time all of the older generation would die, except for Caleb and Joshua who would live to enter the land that God had promised to Abraham and his descendants (Numbers 14:29–33).

More than two generations later, after Joshua led the Israelites to conquer the land, Caleb received the city of Hebron as a reward for his faithfulness (Joshua 14:6–14).

**Learn More:** Deuteronomy 1:35–36 / 1 Chronicles 4:15 / Joshua 15:13–19

# CANAAN

*And Noah awoke from his wine, and knew
what his younger son had done unto him.
And he said, Cursed be Canaan; a servant
of servants shall he be unto his brethren.*
GENESIS 9:24–25

Canaan, a grandson of Noah, was born to Ham, one of Noah's three sons. After sleeping off an unfortunate episode of drunkenness, Noah realized that Ham had seen his nude body while he was asleep, so he cursed Ham's son Canaan. Noah declared that Canaan's offspring would serve the descendants of his other two sons—Shem and Japheth—who had covered him without looking at his nakedness (Genesis 9:18–29).

Canaan's descendants were apparently widespread throughout the ancient world, in places including Babylon and Phoenicia (Genesis 10:6–20). But over time, Canaan's name was attached to the Canaanites, pagan inhabitants of the territory that God promised to Abraham and his descendants.

Canaan's descendants and the tribes into which they developed are familiar names to readers of the Old Testament: Jebusites, Amorites, Girgashites, Hivites, Arkites, Sinites, Arvadites, Zemarites, and Hamathites.

**Learn More:** 1 Chronicles 1:13–16

# CLEOPAS

*And the one of them, whose name was Cleopas,
answering said unto him, Art thou only a stranger
in Jerusalem, and hast not known the things
which are come to pass there in these days?*
LUKE 24:18

Cleopas and an unnamed friend—both followers of Jesus—were walking from Jerusalem to their home in Emmaus. They were discussing rumors they had heard about Jesus' resurrection that had happened that very day (Luke 24:13–32).

Jesus himself joined the two on the road, but they did not recognize Him. This "stranger" explained that the resurrection was a reality, and that it had happened exactly as foretold in Old Testament prophecies.

When Cleopas and his friend reached their destination, Jesus joined them for a meal. As He offered a blessing, He revealed himself to them and then disappeared. The two believers rushed back to Jerusalem to tell the disciples they had seen the resurrected Lord. Suddenly Jesus appeared among them, and they thought they were seeing a ghost. But Jesus calmed their fears and assured them He was more than a spirit by inviting them to touch His body.

**Learn More:** Luke 24:33–48

# CORNELIUS

Cornelius, a Roman military officer, was praying for spiritual guidance when an angel appeared to him in a vision. The angel told him to send for the apostle Peter, who could help him find answers to his spiritual questions.

Meanwhile, Peter was having a vision of his own in the coastal city of Joppa, about thirty-five miles away. Through a vision of clean and unclean animals, the Lord revealed to the apostle that all people, Gentiles as well as Jews, were equal in God's sight (Acts 10:1–43).

Peter accompanied the messengers sent by Cornelius back to Caesarea, where the Roman officer lived. Here the apostle preached the gospel to him and other people who had gathered at the centurion's house. Cornelius and many of these people professed their faith in Jesus and were baptized (Acts 10:44–48).

Up to this event, the gospel had been presented mainly to Jews. But the conversion of Cornelius and his Gentile friends showed clearly that everyone was included in the "whosoever will" of the gospel.

Peter may have had Cornelius's conversion in mind in his speech before the Jerusalem Council. This group of church leaders met to decide whether Gentiles could become Christians without going through the Jewish rite of circumcision. Peter declared that God accepted Gentiles "by giving them the Holy Spirit, just as he did to us" (Acts 15:8 NLT).

# CYRUS

Cyrus was a pagan king whom God used as an instrument of blessing for His people. This ruler over Persia allowed the Jewish exiles to go back to Jerusalem to rebuild their homeland (2 Chronicles 36:22–23).

When Cyrus issued his decree, several decades had gone by since the Babylonians had sacked Jerusalem and taken Israel's most influential people into exile. These captives passed into the hands of Cyrus when Persia defeated Babylon and became the dominant power of the ancient world.

In contrast to the Babylonians, Cyrus treated the Jews and other subject nations with respect. He divided his empire into districts and appointed governors to watch over these territories. His goal was to generate tax revenue from all points of his empire for the Persian treasury.

Cyrus reasoned that allowing his subjects to observe their own religious customs would generate goodwill and prosperity for his government. So he returned the valuables from the temple that the Babylonians had claimed as spoils of war.

**Learn More:** Ezra 1:7–11; 2:1–2 / Isaiah 44:28; 45:1

# DANIEL

*And he [the angel Gabriel]. . .said,
O Daniel, I am now come forth to
give thee skill and understanding.*
DANIEL 9:22

The prophet Daniel was taken into captivity when the nation of Judah fell to the Babylonian army. He, along with three friends—Shadrach, Meshach, and Abednego—was selected as a trainee for service in the administration of the king of Babylon.

Daniel and his friends refused to eat the rich food provided by the king as part of their training regimen. But they flourished on the food they were accustomed to eating. This showed their commitment to the Lord and the Jewish dietary restrictions He had commanded (Daniel 1:5–20).

Daniel's faith was also tested when he was thrown into a den of lions for refusing to pay homage to the king of Babylon as a god. The prophet emerged unharmed after spending a night among these savage beasts (Daniel 6:26; see 6:13–28).

Daniel's most famous prediction is his "seventy weeks" prophecy. It refers to a period of 490 years, or seventy times seven (Daniel 9:20–27). Some interpreters see this as a reference to the time in history when Jesus the Messiah would appear. This happened with the birth of Jesus about 490 years after the exile came to an end.

**Learn More:** Daniel 5:1–31; 7:1–28 / Matthew 24:15

# DAVID

*Then said David to the Philistine, Thou comest to me with a sword, and with a spear, and with a shield: but I come to thee in the name of the LORD of hosts, the God of the armies of Israel, whom thou hast defied.*

1 SAMUEL 17:45

After King Saul disobeyed God, David was anointed as the second king of Israel. His godly character and wise leadership established him as the standard against which all future Jewish kings would be judged (see, for example, 2 Kings 14:1–3).

When just a boy, David killed the giant warrior Goliath of the Philistines, a people at war with Israel (1 Samuel 17:50). King Saul then made David his armor bearer; he eventually became a commander in Saul's army. His popularity in Israel turned Saul against him (1 Samuel 18:5–11), so David fled into the wilderness for several years.

Upon Saul's death, David became king over Israel's southern territory (2 Samuel 2:4). He eventually united the twelve tribes, becoming the undisputed king over all Israel. He captured Jerusalem and turned it into his capital (2 Samuel 5:1–9).

The major blot on David's record was his adulterous affair with Bathsheba and the murder of her husband to cover his crime. Although David confessed his sin and was restored by the Lord, the consequences would break his heart. Still, God had promised David that one of his descendants would always occupy the throne of Israel. The promise was fulfilled in one sense through the offspring who succeeded him. In a spiritual sense, Jesus fulfilled this promise as the Messiah from David's family line (Luke 18:38; see also Matthew 1:1).

**Learn More:** 2 Samuel 17–18 / 1 Kings 1:1–39 / 1 Chronicles 3:1–9; 11:1–9; 17:1–11 / Acts 13:22

# DEBORAH

*And Deborah, a prophetess, the wife of*
*Lapidoth, she judged Israel at that time.*
JUDGES 4:4

Deborah was a unique combination of judge, prophetess, and military deliverer. As a prophetess, she told an Israelite leader named Barak that the time was right for him to defeat their Canaanite oppressors.

Barak answered that he would lead the battle only if Deborah went with him. This shows that she was well-known and highly respected among her people. As a judge or mediator, she heard cases brought by members of her clan at a landmark known as the palm tree of Deborah (Judges 4:5).

Deborah agreed to go with Barak, and this solidified her role as a military deliverer of Israel. She is the only woman among the thirteen deliverers who came to Israel's rescue during the period of the judges. God brought victory to the Israelites by sending a rainstorm that caused the Kishon River to overflow, sweeping away the Canaanite chariots (Judges 5:21).

After Deborah and Barak defeated the Canaanites, she led a song of praise to the Lord for giving them victory over their enemies (Judges 5:1–31).

**Learn More:** Judges 4:1–10

# DORCAS

*Now there was at Joppa a certain disciple
named Tabitha, which by interpretation is
called Dorcas: this woman was full of good
works and almsdeeds which she did.*
ACTS 9:36

The apostle Peter was preaching near the city of Joppa on the Mediterranean coast. Several believers approached him with the news that a kind believer named Dorcas had just died. She had been known for helping the poor widows of the area, particularly for making clothing for them. Dorcas was also known by her Aramaic name, Tabitha.

Taking Dorcas by the hand, Peter said simply, "Tabitha, arise" (Acts 9:40; see 9:36–42). This scene is similar to Jesus' raising of the daughter of Jairus. He used almost the same words to bring her back to life: "Little girl, I say to you, get up" (Mark 5:41 NIV).

At Peter's command, Dorcas opened her eyes and sat up. Then the apostle presented her to the believers and the widows who had been grieving over her death. News of this miracle spread throughout the region, and many people turned to the Lord.

Dorcas may have been converted under the ministry of Philip the evangelist. He had preached in several cities along the coast of the Mediterranean Sea several years before (Acts 8:40).

# ELI

*Now the sons of Eli were sons
of Belial; they knew not the Lord.*
1 SAMUEL 2:12

Samuel's mother, Hannah, took him to live with Eli, high priest of Israel, when Samuel was very young. She had promised to dedicate the boy to the Lord if He would allow her to conceive and give birth to a child (1 Samuel 1:22–28).

As he grew up, Samuel saw what was going on behind the scenes in the high priest's household. Eli's sons were using their authority as priests to take meat from sacrificial offerings before it was fully dedicated to the Lord. Even worse, they were seducing unsuspecting women who gathered at the tabernacle for worship and prayer.

But Eli took no action to discipline his sons, so a prophet warned him that God would judge the entire family severely if the wrongdoing continued. Finally, even the boy Samuel told Eli about a dream he had experienced in which God vowed to judge Eli's family "because of the sin he knew about" (1 Samuel 3:13 NIV).

God's punishment came when Eli's sons were killed in a battle with the Philistines. The news was such a shock that the aged priest fell backward off his chair, and died from a broken neck (1 Samuel 4:18).

**Learn More:** 1 Kings 2:27

# ELIJAH

*And Elijah. . .said, How long halt ye between two opinions? if the LORD be God, follow him: but if Baal, then follow him. And the people answered him not a word.*
1 KINGS 18:21

The prophet Elijah is best known for his dramatic encounter with the prophets of the false god Baal. God proved through this contest that He was the one true God. Then Elijah ordered the execution of these false prophets (1 Kings 18:21–40). This kindled the wrath of Jezebel, wife of King Ahab of Israel, and Elijah had to hide in the wilderness (1 Kings 19:1–4).

Elijah also clashed with King Ahab and his son and successor, Ahaziah, on several occasions. The prophet pronounced God's judgment against Ahab for stealing Naboth's land and having him framed and executed (1 Kings 21:1–24).

As Elijah's ministry wound down, he anointed Elisha as his successor (1 Kings 19:16). Then Elijah was carried bodily into heaven without experiencing physical death. Elisha took Elijah's robe as he ascended to show that his prophetic ministry would continue (2 Kings 2:1–14).

The prophet Malachi predicted that the Lord would send Elijah back to earth before the arrival of the Messiah (Malachi 4:5). This prophecy came to pass in a spiritual sense with the preaching of John the Baptist, forerunner of Jesus. John's lifestyle and preaching were similar to Elijah's (Matthew 17:10–13; *Elias:* KJV).

**Learn More:** 1 Kings 19:15–16 / 2 Kings 1:2–15 / Matthew 17:1–8 / Luke 9:8

# ELISABETH

*And it came to pass, that, when Elisabeth
heard the salutation of Mary, the babe
leaped in her womb; and Elisabeth
was filled with the Holy Ghost.*
LUKE 1:41

Elisabeth was beyond the age when a woman would normally give birth to a child. Imagine her surprise when she discovered she would become a mother. This had been revealed to her husband, Zacharias, by an angel while he performed his duties as a priest in the temple in Jerusalem (Luke 1:5–24).

After Elisabeth conceived, she went into seclusion for five months. During this time she was visited by her relative Mary, who was also expecting a child. When Elisabeth greeted Mary, the baby in Elisabeth's womb moved, as if to honor the child whom Mary was carrying (Luke 1:39–45).

This slight move was prophetic. Elisabeth's son grew up to become John the Baptist, forerunner of Mary's son—Jesus the Messiah. (See also *Zacharias*.)

Elisabeth had been carrying her child for six months when Mary came to visit (Luke 1:36). Since Mary stayed on as Elisabeth's guest for three months (Luke 1:56), it's possible Mary had gone to help her relative during the final months of her pregnancy.

**Learn More:** Luke 1:57–60

# ELISHA

*And he [Elisha]. . .stretched himself upon the child; and the flesh of the child waxed warm.*
2 KINGS 4:34

Elisha ministered in the northern kingdom of Israel during the days of the prophet Elijah. When Elisha realized he was destined to succeed this great prophet, he asked for a double portion of Elijah's spirit to be given to him (2 Kings 2:9).

God granted this request, and Elisha went on to become the greatest miracle worker in the Old Testament. More than a dozen of these miracles are recorded in the book of 2 Kings. He purified the bad waters of a spring (2 Kings 2:19–22), provided a destitute widow with a supply of oil that never had to be replenished (2 Kings 4:1–7), provided food for one hundred prophets (2 Kings 4:42–44), and healed a Syrian military officer (2 Kings 5:1–27).

Elisha was not as active in political matters as Elijah had been. But he did cause soldiers of the Syrian army to go blind to prevent their attacks against Israel (2 Kings 6:18–23). The prophet also played a role in the miraculous deliverance of the city of Samaria from a siege by the Assyrians (2 Kings 7:1–20).

**Learn More:** 2 Kings 8:7–15 / Luke 4:27; *Eliseus:* KJV

# ELYMAS

*But Elymas the sorcerer (for so is his name
by interpretation) withstood them, seeking
to turn away the deputy from the faith.*
ACTS 13:8

Elymas provides proof that some people will oppose God's plan of salvation—but that God will still reach those He intends to save. On the island of Cyprus, the missionaries Paul and Barnabas were meeting in Paphos with the Roman proconsul, a "prudent" (*intelligent*, NIV) man named Sergius Paulus. He had called for Paul and Barnabas specifically to hear God's word. But the governor's attendant, described as a Jewish sorcerer and false prophet called Bar-Jesus or Elymas, interfered, trying to keep his boss from the faith.

Paul, "filled with the Holy Ghost," gave Elymas a public dressing down, telling him, "thou child of the devil, thou enemy of all righteousness, wilt thou not cease to pervert the right ways of the Lord?" (Acts 13:10). When Paul called a temporary blindness on Elymas, Sergius Paulus, "astonished at the doctrine of the Lord," believed Paul's teaching (verse 12).

**Learn More:** Acts 13:4–12

# ENOCH

A person who "walked" with God was known for his steady, consistent relationship to the Lord—a daily pattern of faithfulness to His will. This distinction of "walking with God" was applied to Enoch's life (Genesis 5:24). One modern translation renders this phrase as "walking in close fellowship with God" (NLT).

This brief mention of Enoch in Genesis also says that "he was not; for God took him." The writer of Hebrews explains this by saying Enoch transported (or "translated") into God's presence without experiencing physical death.

Enoch lived for 365 years before this translation experience. He was the father of Methuselah, who lived for 969 years—longer than any other person mentioned in the Bible. Enoch is listed in Luke's genealogy of Jesus in the New Testament (Luke 3:37).

The righteous man Noah, who obeyed God and built an ark to escape the great flood, is also said to have walked with God (Genesis 6:9).

**Learn More:** Jude 14

# ESAU

*And the first [Esau] came out red, all over like an*
*hairy garment; and they called his name Esau.*
GENESIS 25:25

Esau and his twin brother, Jacob, seemed to be destined for
disagreement from the day they were born. Esau emerged
first from the womb of his mother, Rebekah. Right behind
came Jacob, who was grasping his brother's heel as if he
were struggling to be the firstborn (Genesis 25:21–26).

After the boys grew up, Esau traded his birthright—that
is, his rights as the firstborn son—to Jacob for a bowl of stew
(Genesis 25:29–34). Jacob also plotted with his mother to
trick his father, Isaac, into blessing him rather than Esau
(Genesis 27:1–41).

Esau vowed to kill his brother for this act of deception,
so Jacob fled into exile. Years later, when Jacob decided
to return to Canaan, he knew Esau would be waiting with
revenge on his mind. But to his surprise, Esau accepted
the gifts he offered and welcomed him back with no hard
feelings (Genesis 33:1–16).

Esau was also knows as Edom, a name meaning "red,"
from the red stew for which he traded his birthright (Genesis
25:30). His descendants were the Edomites, a tribal group
that lived in an area near the Dead Sea.

**Learn More:** Genesis 35:29; 36:1–19 / Romans 9:12–13

# ESTHER

*Then Esther bade them return Mordecai this answer. . .so will I go in unto the king, which is not according to the law: and if I perish, I perish.*
ESTHER 4:15–16

Esther's story begins in Persia, where she lived with her cousin Mordecai. He had adopted her as a child when both her parents died (Esther 2:5–7). Through a combination of miraculous circumstances, Esther became queen of the Persian Empire when King Ahasuerus deposed his original wife and queen for disobeying one of his orders (Esther 2:12–17).

Later, the king's chief aide, Haman, convinced Ahasuerus to issue a decree authorizing the execution of all Jewish subjects throughout his empire. This was Haman's way of venting his wrath against Mordecai, a minor official in the royal palace. Mordecai had refused to bow before Haman and pay him the respect Haman thought he deserved (Esther 3:5–13).

But Mordecai and Esther acted swiftly and created a plan of their own to save their people. Esther used her influence with the king to expose Haman's plot and have him executed (Esther 7:3–10). Then she had Ahasuerus issue another decree giving the Jews permission to defend themselves on the day of their planned mass execution (Esther 8:3–11). See also *Mordecai*.

**Learn More:** Esther 9:31–32

# EUTYCHUS

*And they brought the young man [Eutychus]*
*alive, and were not a little comforted.*
ACTS 20:12

Anyone who has ever drifted off during a long speech can sympathize with a young man named Eutychus, a believer in the city of Troas.

Eutychus was with other believers on the third floor of a private home. He was listening to a sermon by the apostle Paul that droned on until midnight. Many oil-burning lamps were being used for illumination, and we can guess that this caused the room to become warm and stuffy, since Eutychus was sitting by an open window. He fell fast asleep and apparently tumbled through the opening to his death below. Paul immediately went into action, though, stretching himself over the young man's body and restoring him to life (Acts 20:7–10).

This disturbing event would have caused most preachers to call a halt to the service and send everyone home. But not Paul. He participated with other believers in observance of the Lord's Supper, and did not leave the house until "after talking until daylight" (verse 11 NIV).

# EVE

*And when the woman saw that the tree
was good. . .she took of the fruit thereof,
and did eat, and gave also unto her
husband with her; and he did eat.*
GENESIS 3:6

God fashioned Eve from one of Adam's ribs to serve as his helpmate and companion. He placed both of them in a beautiful garden with all kinds of delicious fruit for them to eat. But He warned that one particular tree was off limits: "You must not eat it or touch it," He declared, "or you will die" (Genesis 3:3 HCSB).

Satan planted doubt in Eve's mind about God's command. So Eve ate from the tree, and convinced Adam to do the same. Their disobedience resulted in the loss of innocence. God punished the couple by driving them from the idyllic garden, and Eve was destined to experience pain and suffering in the process of childbirth (Genesis 3:16).

In the New Testament, the apostle Paul declared that he feared the believers at Corinth would be led astray "just as Eve was deceived by the cunning ways of the serpent" (2 Corinthians 11:3 NLT). Thus, she is an example of the power of temptation and how easily a person can slip into sin. See also *Adam*.

**Learn More:** 1 Timothy 2:12–14

# EZEKIEL

*The word of the LORD came expressly unto
Ezekiel the priest, the son of Buzi, in the land
of the Chaldeans by the river Chebar; and the
hand of the LORD was there upon him.*

EZEKIEL 1:3

Ezekiel was taken into exile with other Jewish citizens when the Babylonians defeated Judah (Ezekiel 1:1–3). Here he apparently spent the rest of his life. He is often referred to as "the prophet to the exiles."

This spokesman for God is also known for acting out his messages through strange behavior, such as lying on his side for more than a year (4:4–6), eating bread baked over cow dung (4:12–15), and shaving off his hair (5:1–4). These actions symbolized the suffering during and after the Babylonian siege of Jerusalem.

Ezekiel's visions from the Lord are also legendary. His call came through a vision of a storm cloud in which mysterious heavenly creatures known as cherubim appeared. God spoke from a throne in the midst of the cloud, commissioning him to his prophetic ministry (1:4–2:3).

The prophet's most spectacular vision, perhaps, was of a valley filled with dry bones. The bones came to life, signifying God's intention to restore His people after their period of exile came to an end (37:1–14).

**Learn More:** Ezekiel 24:1–24

# EZRA

*For Ezra had prepared his heart to seek the
law of the LORD, and to do it, and to teach
in Israel statutes and judgments.*
EZRA 7:10

Ezra was a priest and scribe who led religious reforms in
Judah after his countrymen returned from exile. One group
of people had already returned to Judah under Zerubbabel
when Ezra was granted permission to take another party
back. Zerubbabel's task was to rebuild the temple, while
Ezra was determined to restore the people's commitment
to God's law (Ezra 7:6–28).

Ezra's mission received the blessing of the reigning
Persian king, Artaxerxes. The king gave Ezra a royal letter
that authorized him to carry out reforms. Artaxerxes also
provided funds to furnish the temple after it was rebuilt.

When he arrived in Jerusalem, Ezra was shocked to
learn that many Israelite men had married foreign women
from the surrounding pagan nations. He launched a mass
movement that convinced the offenders to divorce these
wives (Ezra 10:1–17).

Ezra also led the people of Judah to give attention to
the Old Testament law. With help from several priests, he
read from the law for seven days to emphasize the Lord's
commands. During this assembly, the people celebrated
the Feast of Tabernacles to commemorate God's provision
for His people in the wilderness during their escape from
slavery in Egypt (Nehemiah 8:16–18).

**Learn More:** Nehemiah 8:1–9

# GAMALIEL

*Then stood there up one in the council,*
*a Pharisee, named Gamaliel, a doctor of*
*the law, had in reputation among all the*
*people, and commanded to put the*
*apostles forth a little space.*
Acts 5:34

Peter and the other apostles were arrested by the Jewish Sanhedrin for preaching that Jesus was the long-awaited Messiah. This religious high court threatened to execute them for blasphemy. Then Gamaliel, an esteemed teacher and member of the court, stepped forward in the apostles' defense (Acts 5:33–41).

Gamaliel's argument was simple: If the Jesus whom they were preaching was a false prophet, the Christian movement would soon fade away. But if they were preaching the truth, he declared, it could not be stopped by human opposition. The full Sanhedrin was convinced by this reasoning, and they released the apostles to continue their preaching.

This Gamaliel is probably the same learned rabbi under whom the apostle Paul studied in his early years as a zealous advocate of the Jewish law (Acts 22:3).

# GEHAZI

*But Gehazi, the servant of Elisha the man*
*of God, said, Behold, my master hath*
*spared Naaman this Syrian, in not receiving*
*at his hands that which he brought: but,*
*as the LORD liveth, I will run after him,*
*and take somewhat of him.*
2 KINGS 5:20

Gehazi, a servant of the prophet Elisha, acted wisely in
some situations. For example, he helped a poor widow get
her land restored by pleading her case before the king of
Israel (2 Kings 8:1–6). But Gehazi's greed eventually led to
his downfall.

After Elisha healed Naaman the Syrian of leprosy, the
prophet refused Naaman's offer of a reward. But Gehazi
saw this as an opportunity to better himself. He followed
the Syrian military officer, who gave him some items that
Gehazi claimed would be used to help needy prophets who
worked with Elisha. But he actually kept the gifts for himself
(2 Kings 5:20–27).

Elisha learned what his servant had done and confronted
him about it. Gehazi made matters worse by lying to his
master and refusing to own up to his sin. Then the prophet
cursed Gehazi with leprosy—the same disease from which
Naaman had been cured.

**Learn More:** 2 Kings 4:12–31

# GIDEON

*And the Lord said unto Gideon, By the three
hundred men that lapped will I save you,
and deliver the Midianites into thine hand.*
Judges 7:7

Gideon was threshing wheat by a winepress when the angel
of the Lord greeted him as a "mighty man of valour" (Judges
6:12; see 6:1–12). Gideon didn't feel like a brave warrior,
since he was trying to hide his grain from the Midianites.
These raiders were driving the Israelites into poverty by
stealing their crops and livestock.

The angel told Gideon that the Lord had selected him to
deliver the Israelites from these enemies. Gideon protested
that he was not up to the task. Only after the Lord gave
Gideon three miraculous signs did he agree to serve as the
next judge, or military deliverer, of God's people (Judges
6:19–40).

Gideon raised a huge army, only to have it reduced—at
God's command—to an elite force of just three hundred.
Armed with pitchers, torches, and trumpets, Gideon's band
crept into the enemy camp at night. At his signal, they
blew their trumpets and broke their pitchers that masked
the torches inside. This flooded the camp with noise and
light, creating panic. In their confusion, the Midianites
actually killed some of their own comrades. Gideon and
the Israelites won a resounding victory (Judges 7:18–25).

**Learn More:** Judges 6:25–32 / Hebrews 11:32;
*Gedeon:* KJV

# GOLIATH

*And all the men of Israel, when they
saw the man [Goliath], fled from
him, and were sore afraid.*
1 SAMUEL 17:24

The boy David visited the camp of King Saul to bring provisions for his three brothers. These three older sons of Jesse were fighting with Saul in a campaign against the Philistines.

David quickly learned that a huge Philistine soldier named Goliath had bullied Israel's entire army into inaction. Goliath challenged Saul to send one warrior against him in a winner-take-all contest. But not one man volunteered to take on the Philistine champion—that is, not until David stepped forward to put a stop to the giant's brash talk (1 Samuel 17:1–58).

The contrast between Goliath and David could not have been greater. The Philistine, in full armor with a shield and a sword, stood more than nine feet tall. David was a mere lad with nothing but a sling in his hand. But the shepherd boy put his trust in the Lord and felled the giant with one stone expertly slung into his forehead. Then David used Goliath's own sword to cut off his head.

The Philistine army fled when they learned their champion was dead. The Israelites pursued them and won a great victory.

**Learn More:** 1 Samuel 21:8–10 / 1 Chronicles 20:5

# HAGAR

*And he [Abraham] went in unto Hagar, and
she conceived: and when she saw that she had
conceived, her mistress was despised in her eyes.*
GENESIS 16:4

Abraham's wife Sarah was not able to bear children. So
she encouraged him to father a child through Hagar, her
Egyptian servant. But even before the child was born,
Sarah became so resentful that Hagar had to flee into the
wilderness. Here the Lord assured her that He would bless
her child with many descendants (Genesis 16:1–16).

At God's encouragement, Hagar returned to Abraham's
camp. But, several years later after her son Ishmael was
born, she was banished again because of Sarah's jealousy.
The mother and son almost died in the wilderness before
God intervened and renewed His initial promise about
Ishmael's future (Genesis 21:9–21).

In the New Testament, the apostle Paul used Hagar's
experience as an allegory of the freedom of the gospel.
As a slave-wife, Hagar represented bondage to the
Old Testament law. But Sarah was a freeborn wife who
eventually gave birth to Isaac, the child through whom
God's covenant with Abraham was passed on. Thus, Sarah
and Isaac symbolized the new covenant instituted by Jesus
Christ and the freedom of the gospel. See also *Ishmael*.

**Learn More:** Galatians 4:22–31; *Agar:* KJV

# HAM

The second of Noah's three sons (Genesis 5:32), Ham and the rest of Noah's family survived the great flood by entering the ark. After the flood, Ham discovered his father naked and asleep in a drunken stupor. Ham told his brothers, Japheth and Shem. These two covered Noah without looking at his nude body.

Noah, apparently furious because Ham had seen him naked, pronounced a curse against Ham's son Canaan. This meant that the descendants of Ham and his son would serve the offspring of Noah's other sons, Shem and Japheth (Genesis 9:18–26).

Ham had four sons: Cush, Mizraim, Phut, and Canaan (Genesis 10:6). Mizraim's descendants settled in Egypt, while the tribes of Cush and Phut apparently lived in other African territories. Canaan's descendants evolved into the Canaanite people of Phoenicia and Palestine (Genesis 10:6–20).

**Learn More:** 1 Chronicles 1:4, 8

# HAMAN

*And when Haman saw that Mordecai
bowed not, nor did him reverence,
then was Haman full of wrath.*
ESTHER 3:5

Haman, chief aide of the king of Persia, had a problem controlling his anger. He burned with rage when Mordecai, a Jew and a minor official in the royal court, refused to bow down and give him the respect he thought he deserved.

So Haman hatched a plot to exterminate all the Jewish people throughout the Persian Empire. Then he convinced his boss, King Ahasuerus, to sanction the plan with a royal decree (Esther 3:1–15).

What Haman failed to take into account was Mordecai's influence with Queen Esther, the king's wife. Mordecai was her cousin and guardian. He had adopted Esther when she was orphaned as a little girl (Esther 2:5–7). Mordecai told the queen what was going on, and she stepped in to inform the king and thwart Haman's plan.

In an ironic twist, Haman was hanged on the very gallows he had built for Mordecai's execution (Esther 7:1–10), and Mordecai was promoted to a higher position in the king's administration (Esther 8:1–2).

Haman's untimely end shows that the Lord is always in control of events, even when evil seems to have the upper hand.

**Learn More:** Esther 6:1–11

# HANNAH

*Therefore also I [Hannah] have lent
him [Samuel] to the LORD; as long as
he liveth he shall be lent to the LORD.
And he worshipped the LORD there.*
1 SAMUEL 1:28

Hannah was heartbroken because she could not bear children. Her distress was made even worse by the ridicule she suffered from her husband's second wife, Peninnah, who had several children of her own.

But when she visited the high priest Eli at the tabernacle in Shiloh, Hannah took her problem to the Lord. She promised that if God would bless her with a son, she would devote him to His service. The Lord heard her prayer, and Hannah did have a son. She named him Samuel, meaning "heard of God," because she had "asked him of the LORD" (1 Samuel 1:20; see 1:1–28).

When Samuel was about two years old, Hannah kept her promise by placing Samuel in the custody of Eli. The boy Samuel eventually became a great priest and prophet who anointed Saul and David as the first two kings of Israel.

Hannah expressed thanks for her good fortune in a beautiful song of praise to the Lord. She was eventually blessed even further for her faithfulness when she gave birth to three additional sons and two daughters (1 Samuel 2:21).

**Learn More:** 1 Samuel 2:1–10

# HEROD

*Then Herod, when he had privily called the
wise men, enquired of them diligently
what time the star appeared.*

MATTHEW 2:7

This Roman ruler over Palestine, also known as King Herod the Great, attempted to put the baby Jesus to death soon after He was born.

When Herod had suspected several members of his own family of plotting to take over his throne, he had executed them. This same paranoid fear of losing power is probably what motivated him to order the slaughter of all male infants in the vicinity of Bethlehem, the village where Jesus was born. The king had learned that a "king of the Jews" had been born in that village when wise men from the east arrived in Jerusalem searching for the young ruler (Matthew 2:1–16).

But Mary and Joseph were warned in a dream about Herod's plot. They fled to safety in Egypt until the king died. Their sojourn in Egypt fulfilled this messianic prophecy: "Out of Egypt have I called my son" (Matthew 2:15; see Hosea 11:1). Even an evil king's best-laid plans could not turn aside the purpose of God.

Herod was known for his ambitious building projects throughout Israel, particularly the renovation of the Jewish temple in Jerusalem. This was a huge project that dragged on over several decades. It may have been underway during the years of Jesus' public ministry (John 2:18–21).

**Learn More:** Matthew 2:19–21

# HEZEKIAH

*And he [Hezekiah] did that which was
right in the sight of the LORD, according
to all that David his father had done.*
2 CHRONICLES 29:2

A king of Judah, Hezekiah reversed the trend toward idolatry that infected his country. He destroyed pagan images and altars, reopened the temple in Jerusalem that his father had closed, and renewed the celebration of religious festivals. He even destroyed the bronze serpent that Moses had erected in the wilderness centuries earlier because it had become an object of worship (2 Kings 18:1–6; 2 Chronicles 29:3–15).

During Hezekiah's reign, Assyria became a dominant world power that threatened his nation. The king made extensive military preparations by strengthening Jerusalem's defensive wall. He also built a tunnel that connected the city to a spring outside the wall to provide water in the event of a prolonged Assyrian siege (2 Kings 20:20).

When King Sennacherib of Assyria attacked the city, the Lord intervened by striking the enemy camp with a mysterious illness. With his army decimated, Sennacherib withdrew in humiliation and defeat (2 Kings 19:35–36).

Hezekiah suffered a serious illness toward the end of his reign. He prayed for recovery, and the Lord granted him fifteen additional years of life (Isaiah 38:1–8).

**Learn More:** Jeremiah 26:18–19 / Matthew 1:9–10;
*Ezekias:* KJV

# HOSEA

*And the LORD said to Hosea, Go, take unto thee a wife of whoredoms and children of whoredoms: for the land hath committed great whoredom, departing from the LORD.*

HOSEA 1:2

Hosea was a prophet to the northern Jewish kingdom, the nation of Israel, during the final chaotic years before it fell to the Assyrians. His name in itself, meaning "deliverance," sent a message about the precarious situation of Israel as it teetered on the brink of destruction. Hosea recorded his prophecies in the Old Testament book that bears his name.

The prophet's personal life also sent a dramatic message to his countrymen. At God's command, Hosea married a prostitute named Gomer. This represented the "harlotries" or sin of the nation in rejecting God. Gomer eventually returned to her wayward life, only to have Hosea buy her back from the slave market (Hosea 3:1-5). The prophet's action of redemption sent the message that God had not turned His back on His people. He continued to love them, and He wanted to restore them to His love and favor.

In the New Testament, the apostle Paul cited the prophet's love of his wayward wife as an object lesson of God's redeeming grace (Romans 9:25; *Osee*: KJV). Hosea's own life echoed this truth more effectively than the words he spoke.

**Learn More:** Hosea 5:1-15

# HULDAH

*So Hilkiah the priest, and Ahikam, and Achbor,
and Shaphan, and Asahiah, went unto Huldah
the prophetess. . .and they communed with her.*

2 KINGS 22:14

While making preparations to repair the temple, the high priest Hilkiah found a copy of the book of the law. This was probably the first five books of the Old Testament. A delegation of religious officials read parts of this document to King Josiah.

The king was disturbed because he realized the people of Judah had turned away from the precepts in this written law and fallen into worship of false gods. So he sent this delegation to ask Huldah the prophetess if God's judgment would fall on the nation because of these sins.

The prophetess had bad news and good news for Josiah. Yes, she told him, the Lord's judgment would be "kindled against this place, and shall not be quenched" (2 Kings 22:17). But the king could rest easy. This disaster wouldn't happen until after he had passed from the scene. Her prophecy was fulfilled about thirty years later when the Babylonian army sacked Jerusalem.

Huldah is one of the few female prophets mentioned in the Bible. Others are Miriam (Exodus 15:20), Deborah (Judges 4:4), Noadiah (Nehemiah 6:14), and the unnamed wife of the prophet Isaiah (Isaiah 8:3).

**Learn More:** 2 Chronicles 34:22–28

# ISAAC

*And God said, Sarah thy [Abraham's]*
*wife shall bear thee a son indeed;*
*and thou shalt call his name Isaac.*
GENESIS 17:19

God's promise to Abraham that his descendants would become a great nation began to be fulfilled when Isaac was born to this couple in their old age. Isaac's name, meaning "laughter," reflects their disbelief that Sarah could give birth to a child, as well as their overwhelming joy that she finally did (Genesis 17:17–19; 21:1–7).

When Isaac was young, the Lord tested Abraham's faith by directing him to offer his beloved son as a sacrifice. But just as Abraham raised a knife to take the boy's life, God stopped him and provided a ram as a substitute offering. This proved without a doubt that Isaac was destined to become heir to the covenant that God had established with Abraham (Genesis 17:19).

The Bible describes Isaac as a person devoted to God (Genesis 26:25) who lived a quiet life of simple faith (Hebrews 11:17–20). He had an easygoing nature which led him to seek peace with the Canaanites in whose territory he lived (Genesis 26:17–31).

Isaac fathered twin sons, Jacob and Esau. Jacob's sons in turn became the twelve tribes that developed into the nation of Israel.

**Learn More:** Genesis 26:1–12; 27:1–40

# ISAIAH

*The word that Isaiah the son of Amoz saw*
*concerning Judah and Jerusalem.*
ISAIAH 2:1

The prophet Isaiah was called to his ministry in a dramatic vision of God. This encounter made Isaiah aware of his sinfulness. But at the same time, he answered God's call with enthusiasm and determination: "Here am I; send me" (Isaiah 6:8; see 6:1–13).

Isaiah spoke God's message to several kings of Judah in the capital city of Jerusalem. He warned that the nation faced destruction by Assyria unless the people gave up their worship of false gods and turned back to the Lord (Isaiah 10:1–10).

The prophet's book is often called the "fifth gospel" because of its emphasis on God's spiritual deliverance of His people. At the beginning of Jesus' public ministry, He identified himself as the agent of God's redemption whom the prophet had described about seven centuries before (Isaiah 61:1–3; Luke 4:18–19).

Isaiah made more predictions about the coming Messiah than any other Old Testament prophet. His most famous is probably the one quoted every year to help us remember the true meaning of Christmas: "Therefore the Lord himself shall give you a sign; Behold, a virgin shall conceive, and bear a son, and shall call his name Immanuel" (Isaiah 7:14).

**Learn More:** 2 Kings 19:2–20; 20:1–19 / Isaiah 11:1–10; 35:5–6; 53:3–12 / Acts 8:27–38; *Esaias:* KJV

# ISHMAEL

*And Hagar bare Abram a son: and Abram called
his son's name, which Hagar bare, Ishmael.*
GENESIS 16:15

Ishmael was the son of Abraham whom he fathered through Hagar, the Egyptian servant of his wife, Sarah. After Ishmael was born, God appeared to Abraham with a special message—this son was not the fulfillment of God's promise to make Abraham's descendants into a great nation. This would come about through a son named Isaac, who would be born to him and Sarah within a year (Genesis 17:15–21).

After Isaac was born, Sarah favored her own son over Ishmael. One day she saw the older boy mocking Isaac. She insisted that Ishmael and his mother be banished into the wilderness. In this barren place without food and water, the two almost died, but God intervened to save them. He promised that Ishmael would also grow up to become the father of a great nation, just as Isaac's descendants were destined to evolve into the nation of Israel (Genesis 21:12–20).

When Abraham died, Ishmael helped Isaac bury their father (Genesis 25:8–9). Ishmael's descendants eventually settled in northern Arabia. Modern-day Arabs claim him as their distant ancestor. See also *Hagar*.

**Learn More:** Genesis 25:12–18 / 1 Chronicles 1:28–29

# JACOB

*And Jacob called the name of the
place Peniel: for I have seen God
face to face, and my life is preserved.*
GENESIS 32:30

Jacob took advantage of his twin brother Esau by securing Esau's rights as the oldest son through a shrewd trade. Then Jacob tricked their father, Isaac, into blessing him rather than Esau (Genesis 27:18–41).

Jacob was on the run from Esau when the Lord got the trickster's attention through a dream. He saw angels going up and down a stairway into heaven. At the top stood God Himself, who declared that Jacob and his descendants would inherit the covenant promise He had initially made to Abraham (Genesis 28:13–15).

Later, Jacob had another divine experience that was even more startling—a wrestling match with the Lord. As they struggled, God dislocated Jacob's hip, blessed him, and gave him the new name *Israel*, meaning "prince with God" (Genesis 32:28; see 32:24–30).

Humbled by this experience, Jacob was now ready to fulfill the purpose that God had for his life. He fathered twelve sons whose descendants grew into the twelve tribes of Israel.

In the New Testament, the writer of the book of Hebrews included Jacob as one of the heroes of the faith (Hebrews 11:21). Jacob is also listed in the genealogies of Jesus in the Gospels of Matthew (1:2) and Luke (3:34).

**Learn More:** Genesis 29–31

# JAEL

*And Jael went out to meet Sisera, and said unto
him, Turn in, my lord, turn in to me; fear not.
And when he had turned in unto her into the
tent, she covered him with a mantle.*
JUDGES 4:18

Deborah and Barak, judges of Israel, won a decisive victory over Canaanite forces under the command of a military officer named Sisera. Before the battle, Deborah—who was also a prophetess—had predicted that "the LORD shall sell Sisera into the hand of a woman" (Judges 4:9; see also 4:4–24).

It happened exactly as Deborah predicted. Sisera fled the battle scene after his army was defeated. He approached the tent of Jael, wife of Heber the Kenite, seeking refuge in what he thought was friendly territory. She welcomed Sisera by giving him milk to drink, inviting him to hide in her tent, and even promising to warn him if any enemies approached. But then Jael killed the exhausted Sisera as he slept by driving a tent peg through his temple.

To commemorate Israel's defeat of Sisera's forces, Deborah praised the Lord in song. She honored Jael as "blessed above women" for her role in the victory (Judges 5:24).

**Learn More:** Judges 5:1–7

# JAIRUS

*And, behold, there came a man named Jairus,
and he was a ruler of the synagogue: and he
fell down at Jesus' feet, and besought him
that he would come into his house.*

LUKE 8:41

Jairus, an official in the local synagogue, was a desperate man. His beloved twelve-year-old daughter—his only child—was at death's door. So he came to Jesus, fell at His feet, and begged Him to come quickly and make her well (Luke 8:41–55). He obviously had heard about this miracle worker who was healing and teaching in and around the city of Capernaum.

Jesus began to follow Jairus to his house. But then He stopped to heal a woman in the crowd with a serious need of her own. Jairus must have thought, *Hurry up, Jesus, or my little girl will die before you get there.*

Sure enough, messengers arrived at just that moment to confirm Jairus's fears. "Your daughter is dead," they told him. "There's no use troubling the Teacher now" (verse 49 NLT).

Jesus ignored their words, calmed Jairus down, and followed him home. Then He entered the house with the disciples Peter, James, and John and raised Jairus's daughter from the dead with the simple command, "Maid, arise" (verse 54).

**Learn More:** Mark 5:22–41

*And after they had held their peace,
James answered, saying, Men and
brethren, hearken unto me.*
ACTS 15:13

James shows the powerful influence of Jesus' resurrection. As the Lord's brother—more precisely His half brother—James was skeptical of Jesus during His earthly ministry (John 7:3–5). But he eventually became a believer, perhaps after Jesus appeared to him after rising from the dead (1 Corinthians 15:7).

In the early years of the church, James emerged as leader of the believers in Jerusalem. He presided at the council which met in this city to consider whether Gentiles could be saved without undergoing the Jewish rite of circumcision (Acts 15:1–22). James expressed in a few words the position eventually adopted by the entire council: "It is my judgment . . .that we should not make it difficult for the Gentiles who are turning to God" (Acts 15:19 NIV).

The apostle Paul referred to James as an apostle—or a special messenger of Jesus—although neither of them was a member of Jesus' original twelve disciples (Galatians 1:19). James was probably the author of the New Testament epistle of James.

**Learn More:** James 1:1 / Jude 1

# JAMES, JOHN'S BROTHER

*And after six days Jesus taketh with him Peter,
and James, and John, and leadeth them up into
an high mountain apart by themselves: and he
was transfigured before them.*
MARK 9:2

James, a fisherman, was busy at his trade on the Sea of Galilee when Jesus arrived on the scene. Working with him were his brother John and two other fishermen brothers, Peter and Andrew. All four accepted Jesus' call to become His disciples after He miraculously produced a huge catch of fish (Luke 5:3–10).

James and John, along with Peter, emerged as the leading three disciples among the Twelve. They were with Jesus at several major events in His ministry—the raising of Jairus's daughter from the dead (Mark 5:37), His transfiguration (Matthew 17:1–8), and His prayer of anguish in the garden of Gethsemane over His approaching death (Mark 14:33–42).

While James was totally loyal to Jesus, his pride and quick temper sometimes clouded his judgment. He and his brother John asked Jesus to give them places of honor in His coming kingdom (Mark 10:35–45). On another occasion, they asked Jesus to destroy an unwelcoming Samaritan village (Luke 9:52–54). Perhaps this is why Jesus gave them the nickname, "The Sons of Thunder" (Mark 3:17).

**Learn More:** Acts 12:1–2

# JEHOIACHIN

*And Jehoiachin the king of Judah went out to
the king of Babylon. . .and the king of Babylon
took him in the eighth year of his reign.*
2 KINGS 24:12

Jehoiachin could not have become king of Judah at a worse time. His father and predecessor, King Jehoiakim, had not done his son any favors by stopping tribute payments to the Babylonians and rebelling against their authority. Now the army of Babylon's King Nebuchadnezzar was preparing to invade the Jewish nation and seize the payments he had been promised.

As it turned out, Jehoiachin ruled only three months before surrendering peacefully to these well-armed enemies. He and the rest of the royal family, along with other leading citizens of Judah, were taken away to Babylon (2 Kings 24:6–15).

The king's peaceful surrender may have worked to his advantage. He was eventually released from prison and treated with respect by the Babylonian king (Jeremiah 52:31–34).

Jehoiachin was also known as Coniah (Jeremiah 37:1) and Jeconiah (1 Chronicles 3:16–17). He is listed in Matthew's genealogy of Jesus in the New Testament (Matthew 1:11–12; *Jechonias:* KJV).

**Learn More:** 2 Kings 25:27–30 / 2 Chronicles 36:9–10

# JEHOSHAPHAT

*And the L*ORD *was with Jehoshaphat, because
he walked in the first ways of his father
David, and sought not unto Baalim.*
2 CHRONICLES 17:3

Jehoshaphat, the fourth king of Judah, continued the godly practices of his father and predecessor, King Asa. Jehoshaphat banned pagan worship and sent teachers throughout the land to instruct the people in God's law (2 Chronicles 17:3–9).

Jehoshaphat also relied on the Lord in military matters. When a huge coalition army of Judah's enemies threatened to overrun the country, the king prayed for the Lord's help. There was no battle to fight when the king's warriors arrived on the scene. A mysterious foe had decimated the enemy forces (2 Chronicles 20:1–25).

During Jehoshaphat's long reign of twenty-five years, the strained relations between Judah and Israel, the sister kingdom to the north, grew more cordial. Jehoshaphat and King Ahab of Israel even joined forces to go to war against the nation of Aram, or Syria. Ahab was killed in a battle for control of the city of Ramoth Gilead (1 Kings 22:29–38).

Jehoshaphat is listed in the genealogy of Jesus in Matthew's gospel (Matthew 1:8; *Josaphat:* KJV).

**Learn More:** 2 Kings 3:6–14 / 2 Chronicles 18:1–31; 19:4–9

# JEHU

*So Jehu slew all that remained of the house*
*of Ahab in Jezreel, and all his great*
*men, and his kinsfolks, and his priests,*
*until he left him none remaining.*
2 KINGS 10:11

Jehu was anointed as the eleventh king of the northern kingdom by the prophet Elisha. The new king was charged with the task of ending the dynasty of King Ahab, who had led Israel to worship the pagan god Baal (2 Kings 9:1–13). Jehu accomplished this by assassinating King Joram, also known as Jehoram, who had succeeded his father Ahab as king (2 Kings 9:22–24). Next on Jehu's hit list was Jezebel, Ahab's wicked queen, who was behind the nation's slide into idolatry (2 Kings 9:29–37).

Once the killing started, Jehu launched an orgy of executions that went beyond what the Lord desired and what the new king needed to do to establish his authority. These victims included the king of Judah, Israel's sister kingdom to the south, and members of this royal family (2 Kings 9:27; 10:12–14), plus numerous male descendants of King Ahab, as well as Ahab's former court officials and close friends (2 Kings 10:6–11).

Jehu paid for his sins by having a large section of his territory fall to the Arameans, or Syrians (2 Kings 10:30–37).

**Learn More:** Hosea 1:4

# JEPHTHAH

*And Jephthah said unto the elders of Gilead,*
*Did not ye hate me, and expel me out of*
*my father's house? and why are ye come*
*unto me now when ye are in distress?*
JUDGES 11:7

Making a rash vow is always dangerous. And no one shows this more dramatically than Jephthah, a military leader in Israel during the period of the judges.

Jephthah was driven into exile from his home in the territory of Gilead because he was the son of a prostitute. But when the Gileadites got into trouble, their leaders approached him in a contrite spirit: Would he please come back and deliver them from their enemy, the Ammonites (Judges 11:1–11)?

Jephthah agreed to do so after receiving their assurance that he would be rewarded with a place of leadership in Gilead. Then he proceeded to raise an army and rout the Ammonites—but not before making a thoughtless promise: If the Lord would give him success in battle, he vowed, he would offer as a burnt offering whatever came out of his house to greet him on his return.

To Jephthah's horror, his only child—a daughter—came out to meet him, celebrating with a victory dance. The brave military leader tore his clothes in anguish when he realized what a foolish vow he had made (Judges 11:30–35).

**Learn More:** Judges 12:1–7 / Hebrews 11:32; *Jephthae:* KJV

# JEREMIAH

*Then the LORD put forth his hand, and touched*
*my [Jeremiah's] mouth. And the LORD said unto*
*me, Behold, I have put my words in thy mouth.*
JEREMIAH 1:9

Jeremiah was set apart as God's messenger even before he was born (Jeremiah 1:5). His destiny was to preach one uncompromising message: Judah was headed for disaster unless the people renewed their commitment to the Lord.

Five different kings of Judah came and went during the forty years of the prophet's ministry. His message was denied by false prophets. He was imprisoned for saying that defeat at the hands of the Babylonians was inevitable. He was accused of being a traitor because he declared that God would use this pagan nation as an instrument of judgment against His people.

But gloom and doom were not the only themes of Jeremiah's preaching. He also offered hope to the people. While they would be brutalized and carried into captivity, they would eventually return to their homeland and renew their commitment to the Lord.

Jeremiah's prophecies of disaster were fulfilled during his lifetime. The Babylonian army sacked Jerusalem, tore down its temple and defensive wall, and carried the leading citizens into captivity in Babylon (Jeremiah 52:4–16).

**Learn More:** Daniel 9:2 / Jeremiah 31:31–34 / Matthew 16:14; *Jeremias:* KJV

# JEROBOAM

*And he shall give Israel up because
of the sins of Jeroboam, who did sin,
and who made Israel to sin.*
1 KINGS 14:16

King Solomon's high taxes and oppressive labor practices led to widespread discontent among the citizens of Judah. When his kingdom split into two factions after he died, Jeroboam emerged as the first king of the ten northern tribes known as Israel. Two tribes, known as the southern kingdom, or Judah, remained loyal to the house of Solomon (1 Kings 12:1–32).

Jeroboam feared that the people in his territory would eventually switch their loyalty to Judah if they continued to go to Jerusalem to worship at the temple. So he designated two cities, Bethel and Dan, at opposite ends of Israel as alternative worship sites. Here he erected two bull statues that looked similar to the pagan god Baal. These shrines led the people away from worship of the one true God—a problem that plagued all the succeeding kings of Israel.

The Lord sent a prophet to tell Jeroboam that his sins would be severely punished. His army was decimated by the forces of King Abijah of Judah, and Jeroboam died soon thereafter (2 Chronicles 13:1–20).

**Learn More:** 1 Kings 11:26–40; 13:33–34

# JESSE

*And Samuel said unto Jesse. . .*
*Send and fetch him [David]: for we*
*will not sit down till he come hither.*
1 SAMUEL 16:11

After King Saul failed to follow the Lord, God sent the prophet Samuel to anoint one of Jesse's eight sons as the new king of Israel. Beginning with the oldest, Jesse presented seven of his boys to the prophet, only to have each one turned down. Finally, Jesse called his youngest son, David, home from his duties as a shepherd. "Rise and anoint him," the Lord told Samuel. "This is the one" (1 Samuel 16:12 NIV; see 16:1–22).

Later, Saul asked Jesse to permit David to come to his camp and play his harp to calm the king's troubling thoughts. Jesse agreed and sent presents to Saul (1 Samuel 16:16–23). Jesse also sent David to Saul's camp to take food for his sons who were serving in the king's army. While on this mission from his father, David killed the Philistine giant Goliath (1 Samuel 17:12–17, 50–51).

The prophet Isaiah described the coming Messiah as "a rod out of the stem of Jesse" (Isaiah 11:1) and "a root of Jesse" (Isaiah 11:10). This prophecy was fulfilled through Jesus Christ, who emerged from the tribe of Judah through Jesse's family line (Matthew 1:5–6; Luke 3:32).

**Learn More:** Ruth 4:17, 22 / 1 Samuel 17:12; 25:10 / 1 Chronicles 2:12

# JESUS

God. . .hath in these last days spoken unto us
by his Son, whom he hath appointed heir of all
things, by whom also he made the worlds.

HEBREWS 1:1–2

The Jewish people had long expected a Messiah. Finally, Jesus was born in a Bethlehem stable during the reign of Herod the Great (Matthew 2:1–2). Conceived by the Holy Spirit and born to the virgin Mary, He grew up like any Jewish boy (Luke 2:51–52). Yet He had an early consciousness of His divine mission (Luke 2:49).

His baptism by John the Baptist, divinely appointed to pave Jesus' way, launched His public ministry (Matthew 3:1–6). He preached and healed (Mark 1:38–42), taught about the kingdom of God (Luke 12:31–32), and sought the lost (Luke 19:10). He ministered first in Judea, then moved north into Galilee, establishing Capernaum as His home base.

As His three-year ministry drew to a close, Jesus disappointed many with His triumphal entry into Jerusalem on a donkey. This symbolized His humility and commitment to a spiritual rather than earthly kingdom.

Betrayed into the hands of the Jewish Sanhedrin, Jesus was declared guilty of blasphemy. Then the Roman governor, Pilate, crucified Him on a charge of treason. But the grave was not the final word: as predicted, Jesus arose from the dead, conquering sin and death for His followers (1 Corinthians 15:57).

Jesus ascended to heaven where He intercedes for all believers (Hebrews 7:25) and awaits His victorious return when everyone will confess Him as Lord, "to the glory of God the Father" (Philippians 2:11).

**Learn More:** John 1:1–14 / Matthew 4:1–11; 6:1–34 / Colossians 1:12–29

# JETHRO

*And Moses' father in law said unto him,*
*The thing that thou doest is not good.*
EXODUS 18:17

After killing an Egyptian slave foreman, Moses fled to the territory of Midian. Here in the wilderness area near Mount Sinai, he worked as a shepherd for a priest named Jethro—also known as Hobab—and eventually married his daughter (Exodus 2:15–3:1).

Jethro visited Moses and the Israelites in the wilderness near Midian after they had been released from slavery in Egypt. He quickly noticed that Moses was stretching himself too thin by trying to solve every problem that came up among the people.

This wise priest advised his son-in-law to appoint leaders who would share Moses' burden of leadership. These associates would help solve minor disputes. Only major issues would be passed up the line for Moses' personal attention.

To Moses' credit, he did not shrug off this advice as the idle words of a meddling father-in-law. He did as Jethro suggested and became a more effective leader (Exodus 18:13–27). Moses invited his father-in-law to accompany the Israelites to Canaan, but he chose to stay with his own people (Numbers 10:29–30; *Hobab*: KJV).

**Learn More:** Exodus 4:18

# JEZEBEL

*Then Jezebel sent a messenger unto Elijah,*
*saying, So let the gods do to me, and more also,*
*if I make not thy life as the life of one of them*
*by to morrow about this time.*
1 KINGS 19:2

King Ahab of Israel was bad enough on his own. But he doubled his wrongdoing when he married Jezebel, daughter of a pagan ruler of Sidon. She influenced Ahab to promote worship of the pagan god Baal throughout his kingdom (1 Kings 16:31–32).

When the prophet Elijah killed some of the prophets of Baal, Jezebel determined to kill him. Only intervention by the Lord, who hid and sustained Elijah in the wilderness, prevented her from carrying out her death order (1 Kings 19:3–8).

This evil queen was also responsible for the death of Naboth, who owned a plot of ground that King Ahab wanted. She bribed false witnesses to testify against Naboth on a charge of blasphemy, and then had him executed. For this evil deed, the prophet Elijah predicted she would die a violent death (1 Kings 21:23).

This prediction came true several years later when Jehu seized the kingship from Ahab's successor. Jehu ordered Jezebel thrown from an upper story window, then trampled her with his horse. Later, only a few parts of her body were recovered (2 Kings 9:36).

**Learn More:** Revelation 2:20

# JOAB

*Then said Joab, I may not tarry thus with thee.
And he took three darts in his hand, and thrust
them through the heart of Absalom.*
2 SAMUEL 18:14

After David was acclaimed king over all Israel, he captured Jerusalem and turned it into his capital city. A soldier named Joab led the assault, and David rewarded him by naming him his chief military officer (1 Chronicles 11:1–6).

Joab led David's forces in several victories over his enemies, including the Edomites (2 Samuel 8:13–16) and the Ammonites (2 Samuel 11:1). In one campaign, Joab placed a brave warrior named Uriah on the front lines so he would be killed. This was done at David's orders to hide the king's adulterous affair with Uriah's wife (2 Samuel 11:14–24). But Joab was not so compliant when it came to David's rebellious son Absalom. He killed Absalom, even though the king had ordered that his life be spared.

Joab's fate was sealed when he threw his support behind Adonijah rather than Solomon as the claimant to David's throne. At David's orders, Solomon had Joab executed (1 Kings 2:5–6, 28–34).

**Learn More:** 2 Samuel 3:27; 20:9–10; 14:1–22; 19:5–7; 24:2–4

# JOB

*There was a man in the land of Uz, whose name
was Job; and that man was perfect and upright,
and one that feared God, and eschewed evil.*
JOB 1:1

Job was a righteous man whom God allowed Satan to test. God wanted to prove that Job's faithfulness was heartfelt, not simply due to the physical blessings he had been given.

First, Satan was permitted to take Job's livestock and servants—and then his ten children. Job continued to worship God. Soon, Satan covered Job with sores, and his wife urged him to curse God and die. Even at that, he remained faithful.

Before long, three friends came to share in his misery. For a week they were silent, but when Job began to speak, they accused him of wrongdoing. Each tried to convince Job that he needed to repent. He defended himself but—aware that no one is completely righteous before God—was confused as to why he was suffering so terribly. Job voiced many moving expressions of faith, including one of the Bible's earliest hints of Jesus: "I know that my redeemer lives, and that in the end he will stand on the earth" (Job 19:25 NIV).

Ultimately, God intervened to demonstrate Job's limited understanding, and Job repented of his complaining. God rebuked the three friends and restored all of Job's original blessings. See also *Bildad*.

**Learn More:** Job 1 / James 5:11

# JOEL

*The word of the Lord that came
to Joel the son of Pethuel.*
JOEL 1:1

The prophet Joel used the devastation of a plague of locusts to call the people of Israel back to worship of the one true God. As bad as this calamity was, he declared, it was nothing in comparison to the coming day of God's judgment if the people refused to repent (Joel 1:3–15). His prophecies appear in the Old Testament book that bears his name.

On a more positive note, Joel predicted that God's spirit would fill His people if they obeyed the Lord (Joel 2:28–32). In the New Testament, the apostle Peter declared that this prophecy was fulfilled with the outpouring of the Holy Spirit on the early believers on the day of Pentecost (Acts 2:16–21).

Joel's book shows that God can sometimes deliver His message in the form of a natural disaster. Not every calamity should be interpreted in this way. But any natural disturbance—whether flood, storm, or fire—should motivate believers to be more sensitive to His purpose in our lives and the world He has created.

**Learn More:** Joel 3:9–16

# JOHN THE APOSTLE

*He [Jesus] saw other two brethren,*
*James the son of Zebedee, and John his*
*brother, in a ship with Zebedee their father,*
*mending their nets; and he called them.*
MATTHEW 4:21

John was one of the first disciples called by Jesus. He and his brother James were tending their fishing nets on the Sea of Galilee when Jesus invited them to follow Him and become "fishers of men" (Matthew 4:19; see 4:19–22).

John refers to himself in the Gospel that he wrote as "that disciple whom Jesus loved" (John 21:7). John was apparently the disciple whom Jesus asked to care for His mother, Mary, while He was dying on the cross (John 19:26–27).

After Jesus ascended to His Father, John worked with the apostle Peter in Jerusalem to call people to faith in Christ (Acts 4:13; 8:14–15). Later, he wrote a significant part of the New Testament—the Gospel that bears his name as well as the three letters of John and the book of Revelation.

John was probably an old man when he was imprisoned by the Roman government on the island of Patmos near the coastal city of Ephesus. Here he received a series of visions from the Lord that he recorded in Revelation (1:9–11).

**Learn More:** Matthew 17:1–8 / Mark 3:17; 5:37–42; 14:32–42 / Luke 9:51–56 / John 13:23; 20:2, 20; 21:7; 21:20

# JOHN THE BAPTIST

*John did baptize in the wilderness, and preach the
baptism of repentance for the remission of sins.*
MARK 1:4

John the Baptist reminded people of a prophet like Elijah
from the past. John lived in the wilderness and urged people
to repent of their sins and be baptized to signify their spiritual
renewal and total commitment to God (Matthew 3:1–2).

Jesus launched His public ministry by asking to be
baptized by John. This request showed that Jesus identified
with John's message and role as the Lord's forerunner.
John was the last of the prophets, while Jesus was the
proclaimer of the kingdom of God that dawned with His
life and ministry.

Some people thought John was the Messiah whose arrival
had been expected for many centuries. But John insisted
that Jesus was the Promised One who would baptize with
the Holy Spirit and bring salvation to sinners as the sacrificial
Lamb of God (John 1:35–36).

John was eventually imprisoned by Herod Antipas for
condemning the Roman official's illicit marriage. As he
languished in prison, John had a moment of doubt about
whether Jesus was the Messiah for whom he had prepared
the way. He sent two of his disciples to question Jesus
about the matter.

Jesus told John that His preaching and healing in the
name of God the Father proved He was who He claimed
to be. Then Jesus declared, "Of all who have ever lived,
none is greater than John the Baptist" (Matthew 11:11 NLT).

**Learn More:** Mark 1:1–8 / Luke 3:1–18

# JONAH

*Now the Lord had prepared a great fish to
swallow up Jonah. And Jonah was in the belly
of the fish three days and three nights.*
JONAH 1:17

Jonah has been called "the reluctant prophet." God called
him to preach a message of judgment to the people of
Assyria, an enemy nation that Israel hated. But Jonah wanted
no part of God's dealings with these pagans, so he fled on
a ship in the opposite direction (Jonah 1:1–2).

As punishment for his disobedience, the Lord sent a great
fish to swallow Jonah, then delivered him on dry land with
a renewal of His original call. Finally, the prophet set off
grudgingly to Nineveh, Assyria's capital city (Jonah 3:1–2).

At the prophet's preaching, the people repented and
turned to the Lord, much to Jonah's disappointment. "Didn't
I say before I left home that you would do this, LORD?"
Jonah complained. "I knew that you are a merciful and
compassionate God. . . . You are eager to turn back from
destroying people" (Jonah 4:2 NLT). Then God reminded
the prophet that His love had no limits; it extended to all
peoples and nations of the world.

In predicting His death and resurrection, Jesus referred
to Jonah's experience of being delivered from the great
fish (Matthew 12:40; *Jonas*: KJV).

**Learn More:** Jonah 4:3–11

# JONATHAN

*And Jonathan caused David to swear again,
because he loved him: for he loved him as he
loved his own soul.*
1 SAMUEL 20:17

The friendship between Jonathan, King Saul's oldest son, and David is legendary. Jonathan went behind his father's back several times to keep his friend safe from Saul's wrath (1 Samuel 19:1–7). Eventually David fled into the wilderness when Jonathan risked his own life to warn him that Saul was determined to kill him (1 Samuel 20:27–42).

Even though Jonathan was first in line to succeed his father, he gave his friend his royal robe to signify that David would be the next king (1 Samuel 18:1–4). And he secured David's promise that he would deal kindly with Jonathan's family when that day arrived (1 Samuel 20:14–16).

Jonathan and his father were eventually killed in a battle with the Philistines. David poured out his grief for his friend in words of deep sorrow (2 Samuel 1:26). After David became the undisputed king of Israel, he brought Jonathan's handicapped son Mephibosheth to the royal palace and took care of him for the rest of his life (2 Samuel 9:3–7).

**Learn More:** 2 Samuel 21:12–14

# JOSEPH, MARY'S HUSBAND

*Then Joseph being raised from sleep did
as the angel of the Lord had bidden him,
and took unto him his wife.*
MATTHEW 1:24

How tongues must have wagged in Nazareth when Mary became pregnant during her engagement, or betrothal. And Joseph, her husband-to-be, was caught right in the middle of this awkward situation.

When he heard the news, Joseph decided to break their engagement quietly to spare Mary any more embarrassment. While thinking about how to proceed, he fell asleep and had a dream in which an angel told him that Mary's pregnancy had happened through the supernatural action of the Holy Spirit. So, the angel told him, he should "not be afraid to take Mary as your wife" (Matthew 1:20 NLT).

This startling message must have been hard to believe, but Joseph accepted it in faith. And so it came about that this decent, godly man became the stand-in father for the Son who had no father but God Himself.

Joseph was with Mary when Jesus was born in Bethlehem (Luke 2:16). He took Jesus and Mary to Egypt to escape Herod's wrath (Matthew 2:13). Later, he brought the family to Nazareth, where Jesus grew up and probably worked with Joseph in his trade as a carpenter (Matthew 13:55; Luke 2:51).

**Learn More:** Matthew 1:16 / John 1:45; 6:42

# JOSEPH, JACOB'S SON

*So now it was not you that sent me [Joseph]
hither, but God: and he hath made me a father
to Pharaoh, and lord of all his house, and a
ruler throughout all the land of Egypt.*

GENESIS 45:8

Joseph had the good fortune of being born to Jacob's favorite wife, Rachel. Joseph was also conceived when his father was an old man, so Jacob favored him above all his other sons. The jealousy that grew out of this situation led the older brothers to sell Joseph to a caravan of traveling merchants. They covered their evil deed by telling Jacob that his favorite son had been killed by a wild animal (Genesis 37:24–34).

Joseph wound up in Egypt, where he developed a reputation as an interpreter of dreams. He was eventually brought before the pharaoh to tell him the meaning of one of his strange dreams—seven productive years for Egyptian grain, followed by seven years of crop failure. Joseph also recommended that grain be stored during the good years to feed the nation during the famine. Pharaoh responded by naming Joseph as his chief aide to supervise the storage plan (Genesis 41:33–44).

During the lean years, Joseph's brothers came to Egypt to buy grain. Some time had passed since they had seen him, so they did not recognize Joseph at first. After subjecting them to several character tests, he told them who he was and forgave their wrongdoing. Joseph considered the circumstances that brought him to Egypt a series of divine actions that saved the lives of Jacob's family. He made arrangements for his father and all his descendants to move to Egypt to escape the famine.

**Learn More:** Genesis 37:5–8; 41:50–52 / Joshua 24:32 / Psalm 105:17 / Hebrews 11:22

*Joseph of Arimathaea, an honourable counsellor, which also waited for the kingdom of God, came, and went in boldly unto Pilate, and craved the body of Jesus.*

MARK 15:43

Joseph of Arimathea was a follower of Jesus. But he was also a member of the Sanhedrin, the Jewish high court that sentenced Jesus to death. So Joseph lingered in the shadows as a secret follower until the day Jesus died.

Then, in a bold act that left no doubt about his commitment to Jesus, Joseph claimed the Lord's body and placed it in his own new tomb (Mark 15:42–46). Nicodemus, another secret follower, helped Joseph anoint the body with spices before it was entombed.

According to Matthew's Gospel, Joseph was a wealthy man (Matthew 27:57–60). So Jesus' burial in his tomb was a fulfillment of an Old Testament prophecy: "They made His grave with the wicked and with a rich man at His death, although He had done no violence and had not spoken deceitfully" (Isaiah 53:9 HCSB).

Arimathea was a small town about twenty miles northwest of Jerusalem.

**Learn More:** Luke 23:50–53 / John 19:38–42

# JOSHUA

*There shall not any man be able to stand
before thee [Joshua] all the days of thy life:
as I was with Moses, so I will be with thee:
I will not fail thee, nor forsake thee.*

JOSHUA 1:5

Great leaders are hard to follow, and this was particularly true in the case of Moses. He had led the people out of Egypt and brought them through the wilderness for more than forty years. The task of leading the people in conquering Canaan fell to Moses' servant and associate, Joshua. He began with assurance from the Lord that He would give strength for the task, just as He had walked with Moses. Joshua encouraged the people with the same message (Joshua 1:16).

The first city to fall to Joshua's army was Jericho (Joshua 6:1–27). Then he defeated Canaanite strongholds through-out the entire territory. When the days of fighting were over, Joshua convened representatives of the twelve tribes and supervised the assignment of land allotments to each tribe (Joshua 13–19).

Near the end of his life, Joshua called the Israelite leaders together and led them to renew the covenant with the Lord. He reminded them of how God had blessed them by giving them this land. He also cautioned them against worshipping the gods of the pagan Canaanites whom they had defeated (Joshua 24:1–28).

**Learn More:** Exodus 17:9–13; 24:13 / Deuteronomy 31:7

# JOSIAH

*And he [Josiah] did that which was right in
the sight of the L*ORD*, and walked in all the
way of David his father, and turned not
aside to the right hand or to the left.*
2 KINGS 22:2

Josiah was only eight years old when he succeeded his
father as king of Judah (2 Kings 22:1). In his first few years
on the throne, he probably had trusted advisors to help
him govern the country.

In contrast to his evil father, Amon, Josiah was committed
to the Lord. He soon began a series of reforms to turn the
nation back to God. He tore down pagan altars and launched
a campaign to purify the temple from defilement and to
make needed repairs (2 Chronicles 34:1–9).

During the construction project, a copy of the Book
of the Law was found. This was probably a portion of the
book of Deuteronomy. When Josiah listened to passages
from the book, he was shocked at how far the nation had
drifted from God's commands.

This book gave new momentum to the reform movement
the king had already authorized. Soon afterward, he
assembled the people and led them in a public renewal of
their commitment to the Lord (2 Chronicles 34:29–32).

**Learn More:** 2 Kings 22:1–20; 23:1–29 / Matthew 1:10–11;
*Josias:* KJV

# JUDAH

*The sceptre shall not depart from Judah,*
*nor a lawgiver from between his feet,*
*until Shiloh come; and unto him shall*
*the gathering of the people be.*
GENESIS 49:10

Judah was the fourth son of Jacob by his wife Leah. Judah became one of the most prominent of Jacob's twelve sons. The tribe that descended from him became the messianic line through which Jesus' ancestry is traced (Matthew 1:2–3; *Judas:* KJV; Luke 3:30; *Juda:* KJV).

When Joseph's brothers conspired to kill him, Judah stepped forward to plead for the boy's life. They decided to sell Joseph into slavery in Egypt instead (Genesis 37:26–28). Later, when dealing with Joseph as a high Egyptian official, Judah volunteered to be held as a hostage rather than his younger brother Benjamin (Genesis 44:18–34). In response to Judah's eloquent speech, Joseph wept openly and finally identified himself as their long-lost brother (Genesis 45:1–8).

When Jacob blessed his sons near the end of his life, it was Judah rather than the three older sons who received the patriarch's blessing. Jacob predicted that Judah's descendants would become the dominant tribe of the nation of Israel (Genesis 49:8–11).

**Learn More:** Genesis 38 / 1 Chronicles 2:3–4 / Revelation 5:5

# JUDAS ISCARIOT

*Jesus answered, He it is, to whom I
shall give a sop, when I have dipped it.
And when he had dipped the sop, he gave
it to Judas Iscariot, the son of Simon.*
JOHN 13:26

Judas Iscariot will always be remembered as the disciple who betrayed Jesus. Toward the end of Jesus' ministry, Judas realized that His enemies were determined to have Him put to death. So he decided to profit from the situation by turning Jesus over to the Sanhedrin, the Jewish high court. For thirty pieces of silver, Judas led them to Jesus and identified Him with the infamous "Judas kiss" (Matthew 26:47–50).

Jesus knew that Judas was plotting to betray Him. On the night before His arrest, Jesus told His disciples that one of them would turn against Him. Then He clearly identified Judas as the one by giving him a piece of bread while quoting these words from the Old Testament: "The one who eats My bread has raised his heel against me" (John 13:18 HCSB; see Psalm 41:9).

Judas was from the town of Kerioth in southern Judea; thus his name, as Judas of Iscariot, was a veiled reference to the place. He was the only member of the Twelve who was not a native of the region of Galilee in northern Palestine.

**Learn More:** Matthew 27:3–10 / John 12:2–8 / Acts 1:16–20

# KETURAH

*Then again Abraham took a wife,
and her name was Keturah.*
GENESIS 25:1

Keturah was the second wife of Abraham; he apparently married her after the death of Sarah. Keturah gave birth to six sons, who became the ancestors of six Arabian tribes in Palestine and surrounding territories (Genesis 23:1–2; 25:1–6).

God's covenant with Abraham, to make his descendants into a great nation, was continued through Isaac, the son whom he fathered through Sarah. So before he died, Abraham presented gifts to Keturah's sons and sent them "away from his son Isaac, to the land of the East" (Genesis 25:6 HCSB).

One of Keturah's sons was Midian, apparently the ancestor of the tribe known as the Midianites. Jethro, Moses' father-in-law, was from Midian. Joseph's brothers sold him to Midianite traders, who sold him into slavery in Egypt.

Keturah is also referred to as Abraham's concubine. She may have been Abraham's second wife, even before Sarah died.

**Learn More:** 1 Chronicles 1:32–33

# KORAH

*And the earth opened her mouth, and swallowed them up, and their houses, and all the men that appertained unto Korah, and all their goods.*

NUMBERS 16:32

While wandering in the wilderness, the Israelites often complained about Moses and his leadership. But a Levite named Korah took this grumbling to a new level with an organized challenge to Moses' authority.

Korah gathered a following of 250 disgruntled clan leaders and confronted Moses and Aaron. These rebels were jealous of Aaron's position as high priest and of Moses' authority in general. The group apparently thought that all Levites, not just Aaron's priestly family, should be able to perform priestly duties (Numbers 16:1–32).

Moses put the dispute in God's hands. The Korah coalition was instructed to bring containers of incense to the altar of the tabernacle as offerings to the Lord. When they did, the ground on which they were standing suddenly split apart, taking them to their death.

Moses then ordered their bronze incense containers to be collected and hammered into a covering for the altar. This would serve as a warning that "no unauthorized person—no one who was not a descendant of Aaron—should ever enter the LORD's presence to burn incense" (Numbers 16:40 NLT).

**Learn More:** Jude 8–11; *Core:* KJV

# LABAN

*And God came to Laban the Syrian in a dream by night, and said unto him, Take heed that thou speak not to Jacob either good or bad.*
GENESIS 31:24

We could think of Laban as something of a matchmaker. He was involved in the marriages of two of the famous patriarchs of the Bible, Isaac and Jacob. Laban gave permission for his sister Rebekah to marry Isaac (Genesis 24:55–67). In later years, he provided sanctuary for his sister's son Jacob, who eventually married two of Laban's daughters (Genesis 29:16–30).

After tricking his father into giving him his blessing, Jacob fled to Laban's home to escape the wrath of his brother Esau. While lodging with Laban, Jacob found himself on the receiving end of the kind of trickery he had pulled on others.

Jacob was promised his uncle's daughter Rachel if he would work for Laban for seven years. But Laban tricked Jacob into marrying Leah, Rachel's older sister, instead. Jacob had to work seven more years for Rachel's hand. Then Laban persuaded his nephew to work for him a while longer, but apparently didn't pay him what he promised (Genesis 31:7).

Fed up with Laban's trickery, Jacob finally left quietly with his wives and possessions to return to his homeland. But Laban pursued him, convinced that Jacob had taken some idols that belonged to him. They eventually parted ways on peaceful terms, with an agreement that neither would take advantage of the other in their future dealings (Genesis 31:45–55).

**Learn More:** Genesis 31:1–16

# LAZARUS

*Jesus saith unto her, Thy brother*
*[Lazarus] shall rise again.*
JOHN 11:23

Jesus and His disciples were teaching not far from Jerusalem when word came that His friend Lazarus was very sick. Jesus waited two days before setting off toward Bethany, the village where Lazarus lived with his two sisters, Mary and Martha. Jesus often stayed in their home when preaching and healing in and around Jerusalem.

When Jesus arrived, Martha met Him with the news that Lazarus had died. Her words amounted to a gentle reprimand that Jesus had not come sooner. "If you had been here," she told Him, "my brother would not have died" (John 11:21 NIV; see 11:1–44).

Jesus assured Martha that her brother would live again because He had the divine power to bring the dead back to life. Then He called Lazarus out of the tomb with three simple words: "Lazarus, come forth" (verse 43).

According to the Gospel of John, this miracle was the last performed by Jesus before His crucifixion. Because it was so spectacular and so close to Jerusalem, the Jewish Sanhedrin stepped up their plans to arrest Jesus and have Him executed (John 11:45–57). Their murderous plans even included Lazarus because his miraculous emergence from the grave had caused many people to believe in Jesus.

**Learn More:** Luke 10:38–41 / John 12:1–11

# LEAH

*And it came to pass in the evening, that he [Laban] took Leah his daughter, and brought her to him [Jacob]; and he went in unto her.*
GENESIS 29:23

Imagine how surprised Jacob must have been: he thought he had taken Rachel as his wife, but he ended up married to her sister Leah instead (Genesis 29:16–28).

Jacob's father-in-law, Laban, was the man behind the scam. He promised Jacob he could marry Rachel in exchange for seven years of Jacob's work. But Laban substituted his older daughter Leah for Rachel on Jacob's wedding night. Jacob didn't realize he had been tricked until the next morning, after their marriage had been consummated. So the cunning Laban got seven more years of labor out of Jacob for the privilege of marrying his true love.

Leah was always the less favored of Jacob's two sister wives. But Leah bore six of his twelve sons—Reuben, Simeon, Levi, Judah, Issachar, and Zebulun (Genesis 29:31–35; 30:17–20). These sons were ancestors of six of the twelve tribes that developed into the nation of Israel.

**Learn More:** Ruth 4:11

# LEVI

*And she [Leah] conceived again, and bare a son; and said, Now this time will my husband be joined unto me, because I have born him three sons: therefore was his name called Levi.*

GENESIS 29:34

Levi, third son of Jacob and Leah, grew angry when a Canaanite man named Shechem forced himself upon Levi's sister Dinah. In an act of revenge, Levi and his brother Simeon killed all the male members of Shechem's clan, stole their possessions, and took Dinah back to their camp (Genesis 34:1–31).

Levi's three sons grew into the three main divisions of the Levitical priesthood—the Gershonites, the Kohathites, and the Merarites (Genesis 46:11). These Levites served as assistants to the priests in the sacrificial worship system of the Israelites. They performed such duties as preparing the sacred bread known as showbread for the altar, slaughtering and skinning animals for sacrifice, and leading music during worship.

At the end of his life, Jacob condemned Levi and Simeon for their act of violence against the men of Shechem for violating their sister Dinah. "Cursed be their anger, for it was fierce," he declared, "and their wrath, for it was cruel: I will divide them in Jacob, and scatter them in Israel" (Genesis 49:7).

**Learn More:** Exodus 6:16 / Numbers 3:17

# LOIS

*When I [Paul] call to remembrance the*
*unfeigned faith that is in thee, which dwelt*
*first in thy grandmother Lois, and thy mother*
*Eunice; and I am persuaded that in thee also.*
2 Timothy 1:5

Lois was the grandmother of Timothy, a missionary associate of the apostle Paul. She probably played a key role in bringing her grandson to faith in the Lord. The apostle Paul commended Lois for her contribution to Timothy's spiritual development.

Paul also recognized Timothy's mother, Eunice, for the same thing. Perhaps Lois had taught her daughter about the Lord, and Eunice in turn had passed her Christian values on to young Timothy.

Lois shows that the Christian faith, while it cannot be inherited from one's family, is a powerful influence in the lives of many people who turn to the Lord.

# LOT

*And there was a strife between the herdmen of Abram's cattle and the herdmen of Lot's cattle.*
GENESIS 13:7

When Abraham left his homeland at God's call to settle in Canaan, his nephew Lot went with him. Lot was also with his uncle when Abraham lived for a time in Egypt to escape a famine in Canaan (Genesis 12:1–3; 13:1).

Later, back in Canaan, Abraham and Lot accumulated herds of livestock that competed for the same pasturelands. Given first choice of the available land, Lot chose the fertile plains in the Jordan River valley. He failed to consider the consequences of living close to the pagan cities of Sodom and Gomorrah (Genesis 13:6–12).

When God destroyed these two cities because of their wickedness, He sent two angels to rescue Lot and his family. But Lot's wife was turned to a pillar of salt when she looked back at the burning city of Sodom (Genesis 19:26).

After the rest of the family escaped, Lot's two daughters tricked him into sleeping with them in order to bear children to preserve his family line. From their incestuous union came two sons, who became the ancestors of the Moabite and Ammonite peoples (Genesis 19:30–38).

In the New Testament, the apostle Peter used Lot's experience as an example of God's power "to rescue the godly from trials and to hold the unrighteous for punishment on the day of judgment" (2 Peter 2:9 NIV).

**Learn More:** Genesis 11:27–32

# LUKE

*Only Luke is with me. Take Mark, and bring him with thee: for he is profitable to me for the ministry.*
2 TIMOTHY 4:11

Luke was a traveling companion and missionary associate of the apostle Paul. Although Luke wrote the entire book of Acts, he does not refer to himself by name anywhere in the book. Instead, most scholars believe, he used the personal pronouns "we" and "us" to refer to events in which he was involved.

If this is true, Luke was with Paul on at least part of the apostle's first missionary journey (Acts 16:10–17), as well as his second journey (Acts 20:5–21:18). He also accompanied Paul on his trip by ship to Rome (Acts 27:1–28:16). Once in Rome, Luke apparently remained with Paul or somewhere nearby while the apostle was in prison, as Paul indicated in his second epistle to Timothy.

According to Paul, Luke was a physician by profession (Colossians 4:14). In addition to the book of Acts, Luke also wrote the Gospel that bears his name. These two books together make up about one-fourth of the entire New Testament. Both are noted for their historical accuracy and careful attention to detail. Luke addressed both books to a person whom he called Theophilus (Luke 1:1–3; Acts 1:1). See also *Theophilus*.

**Learn More:** Philemon 24; *Lucas*: KJV

# LYDIA

*And a certain woman named Lydia, a seller
of purple, of the city of Thyatira, which
worshipped God, heard us: whose heart the
Lord opened, that she attended unto the
things which were spoken of Paul.*

ACTS 16:14

The apostle Paul was on his second missionary journey with
Timothy and Silas when they stopped at the city of Philippi.
On the Sabbath they went to a nearby river, seeking people
who might be open to the Gospel.

Here they found several women who had apparently
gathered to pray. Among them was a woman named Lydia,
a seller of cloth colored with a purple dye. She paid careful
attention to Paul's presentation of the Gospel, turned to
the Lord, and was baptized. Members of her household
followed her in placing their faith in Jesus (Acts 16:13–15).

Lydia was probably the first convert to Christianity
in Philippi, and thus a member of the church that Paul
founded here. At her invitation, he and his missionary
associates stayed at her house while ministering in the
city (Acts 16:40).

# MALACHI

*The burden of the word of the*
*Lord to Israel by Malachi.*
MALACHI 1:1

The prophet Malachi was one of God's messenger to His people after they returned to Judah from their exile in Babylon and Persia.

At first the people of Judah were enthusiastic about rebuilding their homeland and restoring their religious heritage. But their zeal soon cooled and turned to indifference. They began to withhold tithes and offerings and to bring defective animals as sacrifices. Even the priests became negligent in their duties. Malachi addressed these abuses and called the people to renew their faith in the Lord (Malachi 2:1–8; 3:8–10).

The most familiar passage from Malachi's book is his encouragement to test the Lord in the matter of tithing: "'Bring the whole tithe into the storehouse, that there may be food in my house. Test me in this,' says the Lord Almighty, 'and see if I will not throw open the floodgates of heaven and pour out so much blessing that there will not be room enough to store it'" (Malachi 3:10 NIV).

Malachi closed his book, the last in the Old Testament, with a word of hope about the future Messiah. God would send a messenger similar to the prophet Elijah, who would announce the arrival of the day of the Lord (Malachi 4:5–6). Many interpreters see this as a reference to John the Baptist, forerunner of Jesus.

**Learn More:** Malachi 1:6–14

# MALCHUS

*Then Simon Peter having a sword drew it, and*
*smote the high priest's servant, and cut off his*
*right ear. The servant's name was Malchus.*
JOHN 18:10

Malchus, a servant of the high priest, accompanied the religious leaders who came to arrest Jesus. In an attempt to protect his Master, Peter lashed out with his sword and cut off Malchus's ear. Jesus told Peter to stand down and put his weapon away—because His arrest and forthcoming death were a part of God's redemptive plan (John 18:3–11).

This incident appears in all four Gospels. But only John identifies the servant as Malchus, and only Luke reports that Jesus restored the man's severed ear (Luke 22:51).

**Learn More:** Matthew 26:51–52 / Mark 14:47

# MANASSEH

*So Manasseh made Judah and the inhabitants
of Jerusalem to err, and to do worse than
the heathen, whom the LORD had destroyed
before the children of Israel.*
2 CHRONICLES 33:9

Unlike his godly father and predecessor Hezekiah, King Manasseh of Judah led the nation into a dark age of rebellion against God. Manasseh brought back all the idols his father had destroyed and even erected an image of the pagan goddess Asherah in the temple. He practiced black magic and worshipped the sun, moon, and stars. He paid homage to Molech and sacrificed one of his own sons to this pagan god of the Ammonites (2 Kings 21:1–9).

God punished the king for these evil acts by sending him into captivity in Babylon. Here he repented and turned to the Lord. His captors eventually allowed Manasseh to return to Judah, where he tried to make amends for his mistakes. But he died soon afterward, and his reforms were reversed by Amon, his evil son and successor (2 Chronicles 33:13–23).

Manasseh's reign of fifty-five years planted seeds of unfaithfulness to the Lord from which Judah never recovered. When the nation fell to the Babylonians in later years, the biblical writer blamed this king for its downfall (2 Kings 24:3).

**Learn More:** Jeremiah 15:4

# MARK

*And Barnabas and Saul returned from*
*Jerusalem, when they had fulfilled their*
*ministry, and took with them John,*
*whose surname was Mark.*
ACTS 12:25

Because of God's grace, failure is never the final word. This is the clear message that comes from a young believer known as John Mark.

Mark went with the apostle Paul and his associate Barnabas on their first missionary journey. But for some unknown reason, Mark left them midway through the trip and returned to Jerusalem (Acts 13:13). Because of this, Paul refused to take the young man on his second journey. So Barnabas took Mark and set off in a different direction (Acts 15:37–39).

This novice believer eventually recovered from his initial failure and became a faithful church leader. Even Paul spoke of him with kindness and affection (Colossians 4:10–11; *Marcus:* KJV; 2 Timothy 4:11).

Mark went on to write the Gospel of Mark, probably the first account of Jesus' ministry to be written. He may have based his narrative on eyewitness testimony from the apostle Peter. Mark was apparently Peter's missionary associate, since the apostle referred to him as "my son" (1 Peter 5:13; *Marcus:* KJV).

**Learn More:** Mark 14:43–52

# MARTHA

*She [Martha] saith unto him, Yea, Lord: I believe
that thou art the Christ, the Son of God,
which should come into the world.*
JOHN 11:27

Martha teaches a valuable lesson about what is really important in life. Jesus was a guest in her home in Bethany, where she lived with her sister Mary and her brother Lazarus. Martha was busy in the kitchen, probably fixing a meal for Jesus. But Mary was sitting at Jesus' feet, listening to His teachings.

Martha expressed her frustration that Mary was not lifting a finger to help with the meal. "Lord, dost thou not care that my sister hath left me alone?" she asked Jesus. "Bid her therefore that she help me" (Luke 10:40; see 10:39–42).

Jesus replied that Martha was busy with secondary matters while Mary had chosen to do what was most important at that particular time—spending time with Him.

Martha had another encounter with Jesus near the end of His public ministry. She sent word that His friend Lazarus was very sick. But Jesus didn't arrive at their home until after Lazarus had died. Martha met Him with words of disappointment that He had not come sooner.

Jesus assured her that Lazarus would live again because He was the master over life and death. Then He raised her brother from the grave with the simple words, "Lazarus, come forth" (John 11:43; see 11:17–44). See also *Mary, Martha's sister.*

# MARY, JESUS' MOTHER

*And he [Jesus] went down with them, and came
to Nazareth, and was subject unto them: but his
mother kept all these sayings in her heart.*
LUKE 2:51

Mary, a peasant girl from the village of Nazareth, was engaged to be married to Joseph. Imagine her shock when the angel Gabriel told her she would give birth to the Son of God. How could this be, she wondered, since she had never slept with a man? But the angel quieted Mary's anxiety by explaining that this was all part of God's plan (Luke 1:26–35).

Mary accepted this news as a divine miracle. Then she visited her relative Elizabeth, who was also carrying a child. The unborn baby stirred in Elizabeth's womb when Mary entered her house. This signified that Elizabeth's child—John the Baptist—recognized Mary's son as the long-awaited Messiah.

When Jesus was twelve years old, He accompanied his parents to Jerusalem to observe a Jewish festival. He lagged behind in the Holy City to discuss religious matters with the learned teachers of the day. When Mary found Him, she scolded Him for causing anxiety, but Jesus explained that she and Joseph should not be worried—because He had been called to do the work of God the Father (Luke 2:42–49).

Mary was present when Jesus turned water into wine at a wedding feast (John 2:3–11). She also looked on as He was crucified. Jesus commended His mother to the care of His disciple John (John 19:26–27).

**Learn More:** Luke 1:39–55 / Acts 1:14

# MARY, MARTHA'S SISTER

*Then took Mary a pound of ointment of spikenard, very costly, and anointed the feet of Jesus, and wiped his feet with her hair: and the house was filled with the odour of the ointment.*
JOHN 12:3

Mary lived with her sister Martha and her brother Lazarus in the village of Bethany near Jerusalem. During one of Jesus' visits in their home, He commended Mary for sitting at His feet and listening to His teachings (Luke 10:39–42).

When her brother Lazarus died, Mary grieved in her own quiet way inside the house while her sister went out to meet Jesus. When Martha called Mary to come outside, she fell at Jesus' feet, weeping. Then, like Martha, she declared, "Lord, if thou hadst been here, my brother had not died" (John 11:32).

After Jesus brought Lazarus back to life, Mary showed her gratitude by pouring an expensive ointment on His feet and wiping them with her hair. The disciple Judas objected to this lavish and wasteful display. But Jesus interpreted this unselfish act as an anointing for His forthcoming death. "Leave her alone," He declared. "It was intended that she should save this perfume for the day of my burial" (John 12:7 NIV). See also *Martha*.

The account of Jesus' anointing by a woman also appears in the Gospels of Matthew and Mark. But only John's Gospel identifies her as Mary of Bethany.

**Learn More:** Matthew 26:6–13 / Mark 14:3–9

# MARY MAGDALENE

*Mary Magdalene came and told the disciples
that she had seen the LORD, and that he
had spoken these things unto her.*
JOHN 20:18

Mary apparently was a native of Magdala, a village on the shore of the Sea of Galilee, so she was known as Mary Magdalene. Jesus healed her of demon possession, and she became one of His most loyal followers. She, along with other women, provided food for Him and His disciples (Luke 8:1–3).

Mary was one of the women who looked on as Jesus was crucified (Mark 15:40). She came to His tomb on resurrection morning to finish anointing His body, only to find that the tomb was empty (Mark 16:1–8).

According to the Gospel of John, Mary was the first person to whom Jesus appeared after He rose from the dead. At Jesus' command, she told the disciples that she had seen Him alive. To prove that Mary's report was true, Jesus appeared to them in His resurrection body that same day (John 20:11–20).

Some interpreters suggest that Mary was the sinful woman who anointed Jesus' feet with expensive perfume (Mark 14:3), or the woman accused of adultery whom Jesus forgave (John 8:1–11). But there is no evidence to support either of these theories.

**Learn More:** Matthew 27:57–61 / Mark 16:9–14

# MATTHEW

*And Levi [Matthew] made him [Jesus] a*
*great feast in his own house: and there*
*was a great company of publicans and*
*of others that sat down with them.*
LUKE 5:29

Matthew was busy at his job of collecting taxes when Jesus stopped at his station. Matthew knew that tax collectors, as agents of the Roman government, were hated by their Jewish countrymen. So he must have been shocked when Jesus called him to become one of His disciples. But without hesitation, Matthew got up and followed Jesus (Matthew 9:9–13).

What happened next was even more shocking to the religious elite of the town. Matthew, also known as Levi, hosted a big meal for Jesus and His disciples. He also invited many of his tax collector friends. The scribes and Pharisees heard about this gathering of outcasts, and asked Jesus' disciples why they were eating with such sinful and unworthy people. Jesus answered that He had come into the world to minister to people just like Matthew and his friends (Luke 5:31–32).

Matthew was a loyal follower of Jesus for the rest of His earthly ministry and beyond. Several years after Jesus ascended into heaven, Matthew wrote a narrative about the Lord's life that we know as the Gospel of Matthew. This writing focuses on Jesus as the fulfillment of Old Testament prophecy. It serves as the perfect bridge between the Old and New Testaments.

**Learn More:** Matthew 10:2–4 / Luke 6:13–16 /
Acts 1:13–14

# MATTHIAS

*And they gave forth their lots; and the*
*lot fell upon Matthias; and he was*
*numbered with the eleven apostles.*
ACTS 1:26

Soon after Jesus' ascension, a group of His followers, including the eleven disciples, gathered in Jerusalem. Peter led them to see that the logical next step was to select a person to replace Judas, the disciple who had betrayed Jesus.

Peter pointed to Psalm 69 as a passage that had predicted Judas's act. Psalm 109, a similar section of scripture, left no doubt in the apostle's mind that a replacement was necessary. He quoted a verse from this psalm: "Let his [the betrayer's] days be few; and let another take his office" (verse 8).

The group agreed that whoever took Judas's place should have been an eyewitness of Jesus' life and teachings during His entire public ministry. The names of two believers who met this qualification were put forward. Then Matthias was chosen through the casting of lots as the newest member of the Twelve (Acts 1:15–26).

Nothing else is known about Matthias. While he was obviously a loyal follower of Jesus, he is never mentioned in the Gospels. And after he joined the other apostles, his name never appears again.

# MELCHIZEDEK

*The LORD hath sworn, and will not
repent, Thou art a priest for ever
after the order of Melchizedek.*

PSALM 110:4

Abraham once battled several tribal leaders who had captured his nephew Lot along with Lot's family and possessions. On his way home from the victory, Abraham was greeted and blessed by a mysterious man known as Melchizedek, whose name means "king of righteousness."

Abraham gave Melchizedek a tenth of all the spoils he had collected. This showed that he honored this man's role as a priest and a fellow worshipper of the one true God (Genesis 14:18–20).

The writer of the book of Hebrews described both Jesus and Melchizedek as kings of peace and righteousness. This New Testament author pointed out that the formal priesthood of Israel was temporary in nature. Priests would serve for a while, then die and be replaced by others in the priestly lineage. But Melchizedek was a priest long before the formal priesthood was established through the tribe of Levi and the descendants of Aaron. In the same way, Jesus' priesthood was eternal and non-inherited.

The psalmist David also described Melchizedek as a type of the coming Messiah (Psalm 110:4).

**Learn More:** Hebrews 7:1–12

# MEPHIBOSHETH

*And David said unto him [Mephibosheth],*
*Fear not: for I will surely shew thee kindness for*
*Jonathan thy father's sake, and will restore thee*
*all the land of Saul thy father; and thou shalt*
*eat bread at my table continually.*
2 SAMUEL 9:7

Although King Saul hated and tried to kill David, Saul's son Jonathan was a close friend. Their bond was so strong that David, after he became king, honored Jonathan in a special way. David brought his friend's son Mephibosheth into the royal palace and took care of him for the rest of his life (2 Samuel 9:6–13).

Mephibosheth needed this helping hand. He was lame from a freak accident that happened when he was only five years old. The child's caretaker heard that Jonathan had been killed in a battle with the Philistines. Fearing for Mephibosheth's life, she fled with him in her arms and dropped him. He had been crippled ever since (2 Samuel 4:4).

King David also granted to Mephibosheth the estate of his grandfather Saul. The king also arranged for a former servant of Saul to manage the property on Mephibosheth's behalf.

**Learn More:** 2 Samuel 19:24–30

# METHUSELAH

*And all the days of Methuselah were nine
hundred sixty and nine years: and he died.*
GENESIS 5:27

Methuselah was a descendant of Seth, a family line known
for its godliness. Beginning with Seth's son Enos, members
of this lineage began to "call on the name of the LORD"
(Genesis 4:26). Methuselah fathered Lamech, who in turn
was the father of Noah, the righteous man who survived
the flood by obeying the Lord.

After the birth of Lamech, Methuselah lived for 782
years and died at the age of 969. This life span is longer
than that of any other person mentioned in the Bible. He
is listed in the genealogy of Jesus in the New Testament
(Luke 3:37; *Mathusala*: KJV).

Many years after Methuselah had passed on, Abraham
died at the age of 175 (Genesis 25:7). The Bible observes
that Abraham at his death was an "old man" who was "full
of years" (Genesis 25:8). But he came in a distant second
to Methuselah.

**Learn More:** Genesis 5:21–27

# MICAH

*Micah the Morasthite prophesied. . .saying,*
*Thus saith the Lord of hosts; Zion shall be*
*plowed like a field, and Jerusalem shall*
*become heaps, and the mountain of the*
*house as the high places of a forest.*
JEREMIAH 26:18

The prophet Micah is best known for his prediction that the Messiah would be born in Bethlehem. This look into the future appears in the Old Testament book that bears his name: "But you, Bethlehem Ephrathah, though you are small among the clans of Judah, out of you will come for me one who will be ruler over Israel" (Micah 5:2 NIV).

Micah's ministry occurred during the reigns of three kings of Judah—Jotham, Ahaz, and Hezekiah (Micah 1:1). Thus, he issued his messianic prediction about seven centuries before Jesus was born.

The prophet addressed the moral decline of both Judah and Israel, declaring that God would judge His people because of their sin and rebellion (Micah 3:1–4). He also condemned the social injustices of his time (Micah 2:1–3).

**Learn More:** Micah 1:8–16

# MIRIAM

*And Miriam the prophetess, the sister
of Aaron, took a timbrel in her hand;
and all the women went out after her
with timbrels and with dances.*

EXODUS 15:20

Miriam, sister of Moses and Aaron, played a key role in several major events in the life of Moses, beginning with his days as a baby. She was probably the unnamed sister who arranged for her mother to care for Moses after he was hidden in a basket on the river to escape the Egyptian pharaoh's death order (Exodus 2:1–8).

Later, Miriam led a celebration after the Egyptian army was wiped out at the Red Sea. She assumed the role of a prophetess and led the Israelite women in a song of praise to the Lord (Exodus 15:20–21).

In the wilderness, after Moses had married an Ethiopian woman, Miriam and Aaron questioned his authority. God punished their rebellious spirit by striking Miriam with leprosy. But Moses prayed for her, and she was healed after seven days (Numbers 12:1–15).

**Learn More:** Deuteronomy 24:9 / 1 Chronicles 6:3

# MOAB

Moab was fathered by Lot through an incestuous relationship with his daughter. Moab's descendants grew into a tribal group known as the Moabites, who lived in a rugged territory along the Dead Sea.

Moab as a person is mentioned only once in the Bible (Genesis 19:37). But the Moabites as a tribe are cited numerous times throughout the Old Testament. Moses died after getting a glimpse of Canaan from one of the land of Moab's high peaks.

The Israelites enjoyed peaceful relationships with Moab throughout most of their history. But when they passed through Moab on their way to Canaan, the king of Moab tried to pronounce a curse on the people through a pagan magician named Balaam (Numbers 22:1–6). The attempt failed when God intervened to cause Balaam to bless the Israelites instead (Numbers 24:1–10).

**Learn More:** Ruth 1:1–4

# MORDECAI

*And when Haman saw that Mordecai*
*bowed not, nor did him reverence,*
*then was Haman full of wrath.*
ESTHER 3:5

Mordecai was the guardian of his orphaned cousin Hadassah (Esther 2:5–7), who rose from humble beginnings to become known as Esther, queen of Persia.

This quiet man of deep religious convictions was a minor servant in the court of the Persian king. Mordecai refused to bow down and honor a man named Haman, the king's second in command. Enraged, Haman persuaded his boss to issue a decree for the slaughter of all Jewish people throughout his kingdom (Esther 3:8–12).

Through Queen Esther, Mordecai worked quietly behind the scenes to counteract the threat to his people (Esther 4:1–17). A previous action Mordecai had taken to save the king from assassination worked in his favor (Esther 2:21–22). Haman was hanged on the very gallows he had erected for Mordecai's execution (Esther 7:10), and the king promoted Mordecai to a higher position in his court (Esther 10:2–3). See also *Esther.*

**Learn More:** Esther 6:1–12

# MOSES

*And the LORD spake unto Moses, Go unto*
*Pharaoh, and say unto him, Thus saith the LORD,*
*Let my people go, that they may serve me.*

EXODUS 8:1

God spoke face-to-face with Moses, "as a man speaketh unto his friend" (Exodus 33:11), perhaps because of his faithfulness and leadership over God's people. With the help of his brother Aaron, Moses led the Israelites out of slavery in Egypt and toward the Promised Land. He is the main character of Exodus, Leviticus, Numbers, and Deuteronomy.

Moses had grown up in Egypt, so he knew its customs and traditions. From shepherding in Midian, he knew the territory the Israelites would have to cross on their way to Canaan. Still, Moses tried to avoid God's call. The Lord quieted his objections with a guarantee Moses couldn't ignore: "I will be with thee" (Exodus 3:12).

Strengthened by this promise, Moses presided over ten plagues against Egypt that finally convinced Pharaoh to free the Israelites (Exodus 7–12). Moses led the people through the wilderness for more than forty years. Along the way, he showed the Israelites God's power to provide food and water (Exodus 16:14–16; 17:6); weathered complaints and rebellion against his leadership (Exodus 17:3–4); received the Ten Commandments, guidelines for the people's behavior (Exodus 20:1–17); and supervised the building of the tabernacle to bring order to religious life (Exodus 40:1–8). Moses died at age 120 (Deuteronomy 34:7).

In the New Testament, he is listed as one of the great heroes of the faith (Hebrews 11:23–26).

**Learn More:** Numbers 20:1–13 / Matthew 17:1–3 / 2 Corinthians 3:12–16

# NAAMAN

*Then went he [Naaman] down, and dipped
himself seven times in Jordan. . .and his
flesh came again like unto the flesh of
a little child, and he was clean.*
2 KINGS 5:14

Naaman was an officer in the Syrian army, but he had a problem that couldn't be solved with swords and spears. He had leprosy, a dreaded skin disease.

Through his wife's Israelite servant girl, Naaman learned there was a prophet in Israel named Elisha who could heal his disease. But he was not prepared for the cure that Elisha prescribed—to wash seven times in the Jordan River. Enraged, the military man declared that the rivers of his home country were better than all the rivers of Israel. "Why shouldn't I wash in them and be healed?" he asked (2 Kings 5:12 NLT; see 5:1–14). His pride threatened to rob him of a cure.

Fortunately, Naaman's servants were smarter than their boss—they persuaded him to obey the prophet, and he was cured.

**Learn More:** Luke 4:27

# NABOTH

*And Naboth said to Ahab, The Lord*
*forbid it me, that I should give the*
*inheritance of my fathers unto thee.*
1 Kings 21:3

Naboth owned a fine vineyard, but it couldn't have been in a more unlucky place: it was located near the summer palace of Ahab, evil ruler of the northern kingdom of Israel.

Ahab wanted to turn his neighbor's property into a garden. But Naboth refused to sell because it was part of a family inheritance that he planned to pass on to his own descendants (1 Kings 21:1–19).

Ahab's queen, the wicked Jezebel, plotted to take the land by bribing witnesses to accuse Naboth of blasphemy against God and the king. After Naboth and his sons were stoned to death, Ahab seized the property.

God sent Elijah the prophet with a disturbing message of judgment against Ahab: "In the place where dogs licked the blood of Naboth shall dogs lick thy blood, even thine" (verse 19). This prophecy was fulfilled when Ahab was killed in a battle with the Syrians. Dogs lapped up the water when the king's blood was flushed from his chariot (1 Kings 22:34–38).

**Learn More:** 2 Kings 9:21–37

# NADAB

*And there went out fire from the LORD,*
*and devoured them [Nadab and Abihu],*
*and they died before the LORD.*
LEVITICUS 10:2

Nadab, a son of Aaron, was part of the elite group allowed to accompany Moses, Aaron, and seventy elders when they ascended Mount Sinai to commune with the Lord (Exodus 24:1–10). Along with his father and brothers, Nadab was part of the priestly lineage established when his father was consecrated as the first high priest of Israel (Numbers 3:32).

But Nadab committed a profane act that the Lord punished with his sudden death, as well as that of his brother Abihu. Their sin was burning an incense offering with "strange fire" (Leviticus 10:1). Incense used in worship was to be carefully prepared to exact standards (Exodus 30:34–38). But exactly why Nadab and Abihu's incense offering was unacceptable is unknown.

**Learn More:** Numbers 3:4; 26:60–61

# NATHAN

*And David's anger was greatly kindled*
*against the man; and he said to Nathan,*
*As the LORD liveth, the man that hath*
*done this thing shall surely die.*
2 SAMUEL 12:5

Nathan was a courageous prophet who condemned King David for his infamous double sin—his adulterous affair with Bathsheba and the murder of her husband, Uriah. Nathan told the king a clever story about a rich man who had many flocks of sheep. But he took the only little lamb that a poor man owned to provide a meal for a guest.

David was outraged at this selfish act. He declared that the rich man should be put to death. Then Nathan pointed out that David was actually the man in the story. He had everything a man could ever want, yet he had Uriah killed and took his wife as his own (2 Samuel 12:1–14).

Deeply convicted, David confessed his sin. Later he wrote Psalm 51 about this occasion when "Nathan the prophet came to him" (psalm title). In this psalm he admitted his wrongdoing and pleaded for God's forgiveness.

Nathan was probably attached to David's administration as a court prophet. He wrote accounts of the reigns of both David (1 Chronicles 29:29) and Solomon (2 Chronicles 9:29). This makes his confrontation of David even more daring—David could have refused to heed his message and had him executed.

**Learn More:** 1 Kings 1:22–40 / 1 Chronicles 17:1–14

# NEBUCHADNEZZAR

*And it came to pass. . .that Nebuchadnezzar
king of Babylon came, he and all his host,
against Jerusalem, and pitched against it.*
2 KINGS 25:1

As king of Babylon, Nebuchadnezzar was responsible for destroying Jerusalem and its temple and carrying the leading citizens of the nation into exile (2 Kings 25:1–12).

Nebuchadnezzar's resettlement of subject peoples in Babylon provided slave labor for his building projects. But he also trained intelligent Jewish exiles for minor roles in his administration. The prophet Daniel is a notable example of this policy (Daniel 1:3–6).

One night Nebuchadnezzar had a disturbing dream that none of his court wizards could interpret. So he called on Daniel to tell him what it meant. The flourishing tree in the dream that was cut down, Daniel told him, meant the king would be humiliated and dishonored as the result of God's judgment.

About a year later Nebuchadnezzar was driven from office. He apparently went mad and lived for a time among animals, eating grass like an ox (Daniel 4:33). Later he recovered his sanity and served as a witness to God's power and authority. Nebuchadnezzar praised the Lord and declared, "Those who walk in pride he is able to humble" (Daniel 4:37 NIV).

**Learn More:** Ezra 5:12 / Ezekiel 29:18–20;
*Nebuchadrezzar:* KJV / Daniel 3:1–30

# NEHEMIAH

*And it came to pass, when I [Nehemiah]
heard these words, that I sat down and wept,
and mourned certain days, and fasted,
and prayed before the God of heaven.*
NEHEMIAH 1:4

Nehemiah was a man of prayer as well as a strong leader who knew how to get things done. A descendant of Jewish exiles in Persia, he served as cupbearer to the Persian king.

Word came to Nehemiah that Judah, his ancestral homeland, was in dire straits. Even though the Jewish exiles had been allowed to return to Judah almost one hundred years before, the defensive wall of its capital city had not been rebuilt. This left Jerusalem exposed to its enemies.

Nehemiah prayed earnestly about the problem. Then he secured the king's permission to go to Jerusalem to lead a rebuilding effort (Nehemiah 2:1–6). He inspired the people to commit to the project, enlisted and organized a workforce, and led them to rebuild the wall in fifty-two days (Nehemiah 6:15).

Religious reform was next on Nehemiah's agenda. Along with Ezra the priest, he led the people to renew their commitment to God's law (Nehemiah 8:1–10). Nehemiah also restored the sanctity of the temple and put a stop to buying and selling on the Sabbath (Nehemiah 13:1–22).

**Learn More:** Nehemiah 4:1–9; 5:1–13

# NICODEMUS

*Nicodemus saith unto him [Jesus],*
*How can a man be born when he is*
*old? can he enter the second time*
*into his mother's womb, and be born?*
JOHN 3:4

Nicodemus was the very first person to hear the words of Jesus that we now know as John 3:16—"For God so loved the world, that he gave his only begotten Son, that whosoever believeth in him should not perish, but have everlasting life." That quote was part of a conversation in which Jesus told the man he needed to be "born again."

A member of the Jewish ruling council called the Sanhedrin, Nicodemus bucked the tide of hatred that the national and religious leaders showed toward Jesus. Nicodemus seemed genuinely interested in the Lord, but chose to visit him under cover of darkness. Later, when the Pharisees wanted to arrest Jesus, Nicodemus stood up for Him, saying, "Does our law condemn a man without first hearing him to find out what he has been doing?" (John 7:51 NIV). In his last appearance in the Bible, Nicodemus provided the spices with which Jesus' body was wrapped after His death.

But the man's greatest legacy is undoubtedly the nighttime visit that prompted Jesus' discussion of salvation recorded in John 3, words that have led millions to Christ over the centuries.

**Learn More:** John 3:1–21; 7:45–52; 19:38–40

# NOAH

Noah was a righteous man in a time when the entire world had become hopelessly corrupt. The Lord told Noah that He intended to destroy all living things with a great flood. But Noah and his clan—his sons, Shem, Ham, and Japheth and their wives—would be spared if he would build a giant ark, or boat, in which they could ride out the catastrophe (Genesis 6:11–18).

Noah obeyed the Lord, built the vessel, and entered it with his family and different species of animals before it began to rain. The downpour lasted forty days, and water covered the surface of the earth. But just as God had promised, Noah and his family were safe in the ark (Genesis 7:11–24).

After the flood was over, Noah built an altar and offered a sacrifice of thanksgiving to the Lord (Genesis 8:20–21). Then God told Noah that He would never judge the world again with floodwaters. The Lord sealed this promise by placing a rainbow in the sky (Genesis 9:8–17).

Jesus compared the great flood of Noah's time to His second coming. Just like those who did not expect God's judgment by water in Old Testament times, many people will be unprepared for Jesus' return (Luke 17:22–27; *Noe:* kjv).

**Learn More:** Genesis 9:20–25 / Hebrews 11:7 / 1 Peter 3:20 / 2 Peter 2:5

# ONESIMUS

*I beseech thee for my son Onesimus,*
*whom I have begotten in my bonds.*
PHILEMON 10

Onesimus, a runaway slave, had the good fortune to flee to Rome, where he met the apostle Paul and became a Christian under Paul's influence. The apostle eventually sent Onesimus back to his master, Philemon, a wealthy believer in the city of Colosse. Onesimus carried a letter from Paul which is now known as his epistle to Philemon.

In this letter Paul encouraged Philemon to treat Onesimus with brotherly love because he had been so helpful to Paul's ministry (Philemon 11). The apostle reminded Philemon that Onesimus was now more than a slave—he was a fellow believer in the Lord. These words from Paul amounted to a strong hint that this Christian slave should be granted his freedom (verse 16).

Whether Onesimus was ever set free is not known. But Paul did mention him, along with the apostle's missionary associate Tychicus, in his letter to the Colossian believers (Colossians 4:7–9).

**Learn More:** Philemon 13–14

# PAUL

Paul, also known as Saul, was a strict Pharisee who developed a hatred for the Christian movement in its early years in Jerusalem. He looked on while Jewish religious leaders stoned Stephen to death (Acts 7:59–60; 8:1).

Later, Paul traveled north of Jerusalem to persecute believers in Damascus. He was converted to Christianity in his famous encounter with Jesus known as his "Damascus road" experience (Acts 9:1–8). From then on he was a loyal follower of Jesus who became known as the "apostle to the Gentiles" (see Acts 9:15).

Under the sponsorship of the church in Antioch, Syria, Paul traveled with various missionary partners throughout the Roman world for several years. He founded churches in several major cities of the Roman Empire, including Philippi, Thessalonica, Corinth, and Ephesus. His witness for Christ came to an end in the city of Rome, where he was detained by the Roman authorities (Acts 28:30–31). Most scholars believe he was eventually released but finally executed during a second Roman imprisonment.

During his ministry, Paul wrote thirteen letters, or epistles, to encourage the churches he founded as well as individuals associated with him in his missionary work. These letters—Romans, 1 and 2 Corinthians, Galatians, Ephesians, Philippians, Colossians, 1 and 2 Thessalonians, 1 and 2 Timothy, Titus, and Philemon—make up about one-fourth of the New Testament.

**Learn More:** Acts 9–28

# PETER

*And Simon Peter answered and said, Thou art
the Christ, the Son of the living God.*
MATTHEW 16:16

Peter is often stereotyped as a blunderer who spoke before thinking. But this doesn't do him justice.

The most prominent of the disciples, he was part of the trio described as Jesus' "inner circle"—Peter, James, and John. They were with Jesus during some of the most important events of His ministry—the transfiguration (Matthew 17:1–8), the raising of Jairus's daughter (Mark 5:37–42), and Jesus' prayer struggle in Gethsemane (Mark 14:32–42).

Peter was the first disciple to recognize Jesus as the Messiah—God's Son, sent into the world to redeem sinful humankind. Jesus told Peter that His church would be established through believers who accepted the truth that Peter had declared (Matthew 16:13–19).

Peter swore he would always be faithful to his Master. But then he denied Jesus three times on the night He was arrested. After being forgiven and restored by Jesus, Peter went on to become a bold witness in the early years of the church. On the day of Pentecost, he preached the famous sermon that led three thousand people to declare their faith in Jesus (Acts 2:14–41).

Peter also played a key role in one of the turning points of early Christianity. Through a vision of clean and unclean animals, he realized that God included all people, Gentiles as well as Jews, in His invitation to salvation (Acts 10:9–15). In later years, Peter wrote the New Testament epistles of 1 and 2 Peter.

**Learn More:** Matthew 14:24–36 / Luke 4:38–39

# PHILIP, THE DISCIPLE

*Philip findeth Nathanael, and saith unto him,
We have found him, of whom Moses in the
law, and the prophets, did write, Jesus
of Nazareth, the son of Joseph.*
JOHN 1:45

Philip demonstrates one of the basic principles of discipleship—that believers are ideal witnesses to their family and friends.

As soon as Philip answered Jesus' call to become a disciple, he found his friend Nathanael, also known as Bartholomew. Philip told Nathanael he had met the prophet whom Moses had foretold many centuries before. To Nathanael's skepticism, Philip had the perfect answer: "Come and see for yourself" (John 1:46 NLT; see 1:43–46).

Later, when Jesus prepared to feed a hungry crowd, He asked Philip how it was possible to provide food for so many people. Philip began to calculate the cost instead of responding with faith that Jesus had the power to work such a miracle (John 6:5–7).

But Philip showed more faith as Jesus' earthly ministry was drawing to a close. He teamed up with another disciple, Andrew, to tell Jesus that a group of Greeks wanted to see Him (John 12:20–22). This shows that Philip's commitment to discipleship had not cooled. More than three years after he became a believer, he was still introducing other people to Jesus.

**Learn More:** John 14:8–9 / Acts 1:13

# PHILIP, THE EVANGELIST

*Then Philip went down to the city of Samaria,
and preached Christ unto them.*

ACTS 8:5

Philip is called "the evangelist" for good reason. He was the first believer in the early church to preach the gospel to people who were not full-blooded Jews.

Philip fled from Jerusalem to Samaria when persecution of Christians heated up after the martyrdom of Stephen (Acts 8:1–5). Under his ministry, many Samaritans turned to the Lord. These people were despised by most Jews because their Jewish bloodline had been diluted through intermarriage with foreigners.

After his Samaritan ministry, Philip was directed by an angel to go to the road that led from Jerusalem to the city of Gaza. Here he met an official from the queen of Ethiopia's court. Philip explained the scriptures about Jesus to the man and led him to accept Christ (Acts 8:26–38).

Philip was then caught up by the Holy Spirit and transported to the city of Azotus, where he continued his evangelistic work. He eventually settled in the coastal city of Caesarea (Acts 8:39–40). He was still there about twenty years later when the apostle Paul passed through this city on his way to Jerusalem (Acts 21:8–9).

**Learn More:** Acts 6:1–5

# PILATE

*Pilate. . .went out again unto the Jews, and saith
unto them, I find in him [Jesus] no fault at all.*
JOHN 18:38

The Jewish Sanhedrin did not have authority to execute a prisoner. So they brought Jesus to Pilate, the Roman governor of Judea, to be tried and sentenced. After questioning Jesus, Pilate sensed that He did not deserve the death penalty. The governor tried to dodge responsibility for Jesus' fate by sending Him to Herod at the next judicial level (Luke 23:6–7).

When this ploy failed, Pilate proposed that Jesus be set free to satisfy the Roman custom of releasing one Jewish prisoner during the Passover festival. But the crowd refused, crying out instead for the freedom of a notorious criminal named Barabbas (John 18:39–40). Pilate finally bowed to public pressure and sentenced Jesus to death. He washed his hands in view of the crowd, to signify that he was "innocent of the blood of this just person" (Matthew 27:24).

Over the cross Pilate posted a sign that identified Jesus as the king of the Jews. When the religious leaders objected, he refused to change it. This was a deliberate insult to his Jewish subjects. *Is this the best king you can produce,* he seemed to say, *a man you hate dying on a Roman cross?*

As it turned out, Jesus *was* a king on a cross, and He held the salvation of the whole world in His hands. "When he was hung on the cross," the apostle Paul declared, "he took upon himself the curse for our wrongdoing" (Galatians 3:13 NLT).

**Learn More:** Mark 15:1–15 / Luke 23:1–25 / John 18:29–38

# PRISCILLA

*Greet Priscilla and Aquila. . .who have for
my life laid down their own necks: unto
whom not only I give thanks, but also
all the churches of the Gentiles.*
ROMANS 16:3–4

Priscilla was a believer who, with her husband, Aquila, put her life on the line for the apostle Paul and helped him in several of the churches he founded. No details about their risk for Paul are known, but it may have happened in Ephesus during the riot incited by Demetrius the silversmith (Acts 19:23–41).

What is clear is that the couple was associated with the apostle in his work with the Ephesian believers. After Paul left Ephesus, they stayed on and instructed an eloquent preacher named Apollos more thoroughly in the Christian faith (Acts 18:18–28).

Priscilla and Aquila also apparently helped Paul in his work at Corinth. They were already in the city when the apostle arrived. He lived with them for a time, and they practiced their mutual craft of tentmaking while presenting the gospel to citizens of the area (Acts 18:1–3).

The couple joined Paul in sending greetings to the believers at Corinth. He wrote this letter from Ephesus, noting that a house church was meeting at that time in Priscilla and Aquila's home (1 Corinthians 16:19).

**Learn More:** 2 Timothy 4:19; *Prisca:* KJV

# RACHEL

Rachel first caught Jacob's eye when he arrived in Haran while fleeing from his brother Esau. He learned that Rachel was his cousin, the daughter of his uncle Laban (Genesis 29:9–12). Jacob stayed with Laban and worked out an agreement to pay for the privilege of marrying Rachel. But Laban tricked Jacob into marrying her older sister Leah instead. Then Jacob had to work seven additional years to take Rachel as his wife (Genesis 29:16–28).

Although Rachel was Jacob's favorite wife, she was not able to bear children. She envied her sister, who presented Jacob with several sons. Finally, Rachel allowed Jacob to father two sons through her servant Bilhah (Genesis 30:1–8).

Rachel did eventually have two sons—Joseph (Genesis 30:22–24) and Benjamin (Genesis 35:16–20). But she died giving birth to Benjamin. Jacob buried her in a tomb near Bethlehem. This tomb was still visible several centuries later during the period of the judges (1 Samuel 10:2).

**Learn More:** Genesis 30:14–15 / Ruth 4:11 / Jeremiah 31:15; *Rahel*: KJV / Matthew 2:16–18

# RAHAB

*And Joshua saved Rahab the harlot alive. . .
and she dwelleth in Israel even unto this day;
because she hid the messengers, which
Joshua sent to spy out Jericho.*
JOSHUA 6:25

Soon after the Israelites entered the Promised Land, Joshua sent spies to determine the strength of Jericho, a major Canaanite city. The spies went to the home of a prostitute named Rahab, probably to avoid arousing suspicion. But they were detected, and a force was sent to arrest them.

The spies persuaded Rahab to hide them on the roof of her house. In return, they promised to spare her and her family when Joshua and his forces destroyed the city. Rahab's conversation with the spies shows she was a believer in the one true God (Joshua 2:1–21). She helped them escape to safety by letting them down over the city wall through a window in her house.

After Jericho fell, Rahab and her family apparently joined the Israelite community (Joshua 6:25). From her family line emerged King David, and eventually the long-awaited Messiah. She is listed in Matthew's genealogy of Jesus (Matthew 1:5; *Rachab*: KJV).

Rahab was also cited for her great faith by the writer of the New Testament book of Hebrews (Hebrews 11:30–31).

**Learn More:** James 2:25

# REBEKAH

*And Isaac brought her [Rebekah] into his mother
Sarah's tent, and took Rebekah, and she became
his wife; and he loved her: and Isaac was
comforted after his mother's death.*
GENESIS 24:67

Rebekah may be the only wife ever selected by thirsty
camels. Abraham's servant knew she was God's choice
because she allowed him and his weary camels to drink
from the well where she was drawing water. Abraham
had sent his servant into Rebekah's territory—Abraham's
ancestral home in Haran—to find a wife for his son Isaac
(Genesis 24:1–28).

Isaac was pleased with the servant's choice from the
moment he saw Rebekah. She apparently was his one and
only wife for the rest of his life.

Rebekah eventually gave birth to twin boys, Esau and
Jacob. She showed favoritism toward Jacob (Genesis 25:28).
She conspired with Jacob to fool Isaac into blessing Jacob
rather than the oldest son, Esau. When Esau threatened to
kill his brother, Rebekah sent Jacob to live with her brother
Laban in Haran (Genesis 27:41–45).

After Rebekah died, she was buried in the family tomb
at Machpelah. This is where Abraham and his wife Sarah,
Jacob and his wife Leah, and Rebekah's husband Isaac were
also laid to rest (Genesis 49:29–31).

**Learn More:** Genesis 26:1–11 / Romans 9:10; *Rebecca:* KJV

# REHOBOAM

*And it came to pass, when Rehoboam
had established the kingdom, and had
strengthened himself, he forsook the
law of the Lord, and all Israel with him.*
2 Chronicles 12:1

Rehoboam was the foolish son who succeeded his father Solomon as king of Judah. Rather than relaxing Solomon's oppressive policies as some of his subjects requested, Rehoboam vowed to make them even worse (1 Kings 12:11).

This out-of-touch attitude drove the ten northern tribes in Solomon's kingdom to rebel and establish their own country. So from the time of Rehoboam on, the Jewish people were divided into two factions: the southern kingdom known as Judah and the northern kingdom that was called Israel.

Refusing to listen to his subjects was not the last of Rehoboam's foolish acts. He also deployed his army to force Israel back under his authority. Not until the Lord sent a prophet to tell the king to stand down did he stop these senseless campaigns (1 Kings 12:21–24).

Like his father before him, Rehoboam also built up a huge harem. Many of these wives were foreigners whom he catered to by setting up shrines for their worship of false gods. The Lord punished Judah's idol-worshipping by sending the pharaoh of Egypt to plunder the temple and Rehoboam's royal palace (1 Kings 14:22–26).

**Learn More:** 2 Chronicles 11:1–22; 12:1–16

# REUBEN

*And Reuben said unto them, Shed no blood,*
*but cast him [Joseph] into this pit that is in the*
*wilderness, and lay no hand upon him;*
*that he might rid him out of their hands,*
*to deliver him to his father again.*
GENESIS 37:22

Reuben was the oldest of the twelve sons of Jacob. As the firstborn son, he would have received a double share of his father's estate and become leader of the clan. But he foolishly committed incest with Jacob's concubine and forfeited his birthright (Genesis 35:22; 49:3–4).

In spite of this poor judgment, Reuben fared better when it came to his half brother Joseph. Reuben saved Joseph's life by convincing the other jealous brothers not to kill their younger sibling. When a caravan of traders happened by, Joseph's brothers sold him as a slave (Genesis 37:19–29).

Later, Reuben and his brothers dealt with Joseph face-to-face when they came to Egypt to buy grain during a famine in Canaan. When Joseph insisted that one of them be held as a hostage, Reuben reminded his siblings that they were being repaid for the way they had treated Joseph years before (Genesis 42:21–22).

Reuben was the father of four sons. His descendants developed into one of the twelve tribes of the nation of Israel (1 Chronicles 5:1–3).

**Learn More:** Genesis 29:32; 30:14; 46:9

# RHODA

*And when she [Rhoda] knew Peter's voice, she*
*opened not the gate for gladness, but ran in,*
*and told how Peter stood before the gate.*
ACTS 12:14

Have you ever been so surprised by something that it caused you to act irrationally? That happened to Rhoda, a servant girl in the home of Mary, mother of John Mark. Several believers were gathered inside this Jerusalem house for a prayer meeting. They were probably praying for the apostle Peter, who had just been imprisoned by the local Roman ruler, Herod Agrippa I (Acts 12:1).

Someone knocked at the door, and Rhoda went to answer. She recognized the voice of Peter, but she was so shocked that she rushed back inside to tell the others without letting him in. This left Peter standing outside, still knocking.

These believers knew Peter was locked away, so they thought Rhoda was out of her mind. When they opened the door and saw the apostle, they were just as shocked as she was (Acts 12:11–16).

The irony is that the believers were so surprised that their pleas for Peter's safety were answered so dramatically and so quickly. Sometimes God overwhelms us with His answer to our earnest prayers.

# RUTH

*And Ruth said. . .whither thou goest, I will go;*
*and where thou lodgest, I will lodge: thy people*
*shall be my people, and thy God my God.*
RUTH 1:16

Although Ruth was a Gentile, her story played out in Jewish territory. It is recorded in the Old Testament book that bears her name. A severe famine in Bethlehem forced a Jewish family—Naomi, her husband, and her two sons—to move to Ruth's home country of Moab. But tragedy followed them there: Naomi's husband died, followed by the death of her sons, who had married Moabite women.

One of Naomi's daughters-in-law was Ruth. When Naomi decided to return to Bethlehem, Ruth insisted on going with her, although that meant leaving her own people. Ruth's words to Naomi, "Intreat me not to leave thee," are often used in modern wedding ceremonies to dramatize the unconditional commitment the husband and wife are making to each other (see Ruth 1:1–17).

Once settled in Bethlehem, Ruth went to the fields to glean—that is, to gather grain left behind by harvesters to feed the poor. Here she met the landowner, a man named Boaz, who was a distant relative of Naomi and her deceased husband.

Naomi encouraged Ruth to follow up on this brief introduction by cultivating a closer relationship with Boaz. This led to their marriage and the birth of a son named Obed, the grandfather of King David (Ruth 4:13–22). See also *Boaz*.

**Learn More:** Matthew 1:5

# SALOME

*There were also women looking on afar off: among whom was Mary Magdalene, and Mary the mother of James the less and of Joses, and Salome.*
MARK 15:40

A follower of Jesus, Salome was one of the women who looked on as Jesus was crucified. Along with other women, she also brought spices to anoint His body on the morning when He arose from the grave (Mark 16:1).

Salome may be the same woman identified in a parallel passage as "the mother of Zebedee's children" (Matthew 27:56). Jesus' disciples James and John were the sons of a man named Zebedee (Matthew 4:21–22); if this is the same Salome, she asked Jesus to grant special favors to her sons in His coming kingdom.

Jesus told the three that the prestigious positions in His coming kingdom would be given by God the Father (Matthew 20:20–23).

# SAMSON

*And the Spirit of the LORD began to move
him [Samson] at times in the camp of
Dan between Zorah and Eshtaol.*
JUDGES 13:25

Samson's parents had great hopes for their son. Even before
he was born, they set him apart as a Nazarite, a person
who would be totally devoted to the Lord. To show this
commitment, he was not to partake of strong drink (Judges
13:7). This vow also stipulated that a Nazarite should never
cut his hair (Numbers 6:5).

Samson grew up to become the last of the judges, or
military heroes, who delivered Israel from its enemies. In
his case, he clashed with the Philistines. His superhuman
strength from the Lord enabled him to burn their crops
(Judges 15:4–5), kill a thousand warriors with nothing but
a bone as a weapon (Judges 15:15), and rip the gate from
one of their walled cities (Judges 16:3).

But Samson's physical strength was offset by his weak
moral character. His lust led him to several encounters with
pagan Philistine women, the worst of which was Delilah.
She betrayed him to his enemies while he slept. They cut
his hair, causing Samson's strength to leave him. He was
captured and imprisoned by his enemies.

Samson performed one final heroic act after his strength
returned. He toppled a pagan Philistine temple and wiped
out many of his enemies. This was also an act of suicide, since
he too was killed by the falling stones (Judges 16:28–30).

Samson is listed as a hero of the faith in the New
Testament book of Hebrews (Hebrews 11:32).

**Learn More:** Judges 14:1–20

# SAMUEL

*And the LORD came, and stood, and called as at other times, Samuel, Samuel. Then Samuel answered, Speak; for thy servant heareth.*

1 SAMUEL 3:10

The prophet Samuel was born in answer to the prayer of his mother, Hannah, who had not been able to have children. In gratitude to the Lord, she dedicated Samuel to God's service and placed him in the custody of Eli, the high priest of Israel (1 Samuel 1:24–28).

Samuel followed the Lord, and he was faithful to speak God's message to others. Even as a boy, he predicted God's judgment against Eli and his family (1 Samuel 3:11–18). Samuel also served in a priestly role by offering sacrifices on behalf of the people and leading them to commit themselves to the Lord (1 Samuel 7:3–17).

At God's command, Samuel also anointed Saul as the first king of Israel (1 Samuel 10:1). When Saul failed to obey the Lord, Samuel selected a new king from among the sons of Jesse. God made it clear to Samuel that David, the youngest son of this family, was His choice as Saul's replacement and successor (1 Samuel 16:11–13).

Samuel is listed in the New Testament as one of the Old Testament heroes of the faith (Hebrews 11:32).

**Learn More:** 1 Samuel 12:1–19; 28:11–19 / 1 Chronicles 6:33; *Shemuel*: KJV

# SAPPHIRA

*Then Peter said unto her [Sapphira], How is
it that ye have agreed together to tempt the
Spirit of the Lord? behold, the feet of them
which have buried thy husband are at the
door, and shall carry thee out.*

ACTS 5:9

In the early days of the Christian movement, the believers
looked out for one another by pooling their possessions.
When a member of the group needed financial help, this
need was met from the common treasury.

Two believers, Sapphira and her husband, Ananias, placed
money into this fund from a sale of their property. But then
the apostles discovered they had kept back part of the
money for themselves while claiming they had dedicated
all of it to help the needy.

The apostle Peter first confronted Ananias about what
he had done. Peter explained that Ananias was not required
to give all he had gained from the sale. It was his money to
use as he wished. But lying about what he had done was an
attempt to deceive the Holy Spirit.

Ananias was so shocked by this revelation that he fell
down and died. Later, the same thing happened to Sapphira
when she repeated the same lie. This event sent shock waves
through the church and everyone else who heard about
it. God's supernatural power was alive and active in the
movement known as the early Christian church (Acts 5:1–11).

# SARAH

*And God said, Sarah thy wife shall bear thee a
son indeed; and thou shalt call his name Isaac:
and I will establish my covenant with him for an
everlasting covenant, and with his seed after him.*
GENESIS 17:19

The wife of Abraham, Sarah was not able to bear children.
This presented a dilemma, since God had promised to bless
Abraham and make him the ancestor of a people who would
bring honor and glory to the Lord (Genesis 12:2; 15:1–2).

In desperation, Sarah persuaded Abraham to father
a child through her servant, Hagar. But God revealed to
the couple that the son of this secondary union was not
the child who would fulfill God's covenant promise
(Genesis 16:1–2; 17:19–21).

Finally, when Sarah was ninety years old, she and
Abraham had a son who was God's chosen one. They
called him Isaac, a name meaning "laughter," because
Sarah had laughed when the Lord told her she would
bear a son in her old age (Genesis 18:11–15).

The writer of the New Testament book of Hebrews
included Sarah among those commended for their great
faith in the Lord (Hebrews 11:11; *Sara:* KJV).

**Learn More:** Isaiah 51:2

# SAUL

*And Samuel said to all the people, See ye him
[Saul] whom the LORD hath chosen, that there is
none like him among all the people? And all the
people shouted, and said, God save the king.*

1 SAMUEL 10:24

Saul had a lot going for him when he was anointed as the first king of Israel. He showed genuine humility and surprise that he'd been selected (1 Samuel 9:21; 10:22), and he looked like a royal figure—tall and commanding in appearance (1 Samuel 9:2). He also developed into a capable military commander, leading the Israelites to victory over many of their enemies, including the powerful Philistines (1 Samuel 14:47).

But not long into his kingship, Saul's true character came to light. He performed a ritual sacrifice, a duty reserved for priests (1 Samuel 13:9–14). Then he disobeyed God by keeping some spoils of war after defeating the Amalekites (1 Samuel 15:21–23). Because of these failures, God withdrew His Spirit from Saul, rejected him as king, and had David anointed as replacement (1 Samuel 16:11–14).

Saul did not relinquish power without a fight. For several years he tried to kill David. He even slaughtered eighty-five priests whom he suspected of aiding and befriending the man who was destined to replace him (1 Samuel 22:13–18).

Facing a crucial battle with the Philistines, Saul called up the spirit of the deceased Samuel to ask about the outcome of the conflict.

The prophet told Saul that Israel would be defeated and the king and his sons would be killed. As predicted, Saul was seriously wounded during the battle. He committed suicide by falling on a sword to keep from being captured by the enemy (1 Samuel 31:1–4).

**Learn More:** 1 Samuel 28:11–20

# SENNACHERIB

*Now in the fourteenth year of king Hezekiah did Sennacherib king of Assyria come up against all the fenced cities of Judah, and took them.*
2 Kings 18:13

Judah's King Hezekiah had the misfortune of ruling when the Assyrians were on a mission of world conquest. King Sennacherib of Assyria captured several fortified cities of Judah. But the capital city, Jerusalem, was the coveted prize that he really wanted.

Hezekiah kept the Assyrian king at bay for a while by paying protection money (2 Kings 18:13–16). But Hezekiah eventually quit paying. Sennacherib sent messengers to threaten the king, who prayed for divine guidance. Hezekiah stood his ground after the prophet Isaiah assured him that God would not allow Jerusalem to fall into Sennacherib's hands (2 Kings 19:1–7).

When the Assyrian army camped outside Jerusalem, it was devastated by a mysterious plague that killed thousands of soldiers. Sennacherib was forced to withdraw in humiliation and defeat. Later, this powerful king was assassinated by two of his own sons while worshipping at a pagan temple in his capital city (2 Kings 19:35–37).

**Learn More:** 2 Chronicles 32:1–22 / Isaiah 36:1–37:38

# SHADRACH

*And these three men, Shadrach, Meshach, and Abednego, fell down bound into the midst of the burning fiery furnace.*
DANIEL 3:23

Shadrach was a Jewish exile in Babylon whose faith in the one true God remained unshaken, although it was tested by fire—literally.

Nebuchadnezzar, the Babylonian king, set up a huge statue of himself that he ordered all his subjects to worship. Shadrach, along with his friends Meshach and Abednego, refused to do so. They declared that only the one true God of their native land was worthy of worship.

Enraged, the king had them thrown into a "fiery furnace," perhaps an ore smelter or brick kiln. But when the king checked to see how the execution was proceeding, he was astonished to see them walking around, untouched by the flames. Even more amazing, he saw a fourth man, an angel, among them.

Nebuchadnezzar was impressed with the power of this divine Being who delivered Shadrach and his friends. He decreed that anyone who spoke against this God would be severely punished (Daniel 3:1–30).

Although they were Jewish exiles, Shadrach and his friends had been trained to serve in the royal palace of Babylon. After their miraculous deliverance, the king promoted them to higher positions.

**Learn More:** Daniel 1:3–20

# SHEM

*And he [Noah] said, Blessed be the L<small>ORD</small> God*
*of Shem; and Canaan shall be his servant.*
G<small>ENESIS</small> 9:26

Shem was the oldest of Noah's three sons who survived the great flood by entering the ark. After the flood, Shem and his brother Japheth covered their father's nudity while he was sleeping off a drunken stupor. They did so by walking backward toward Noah so they would not see his naked body (Genesis 9:18–27).

After Noah woke up, he was pleased with Shem's actions to cover him up. He blessed Shem and declared that the descendants of Noah's third son, Ham, would be servants of Shem and his offspring. Noah was angry with Ham because he had seen his father's nakedness before notifying his two brothers.

Shem was the father of several sons whose descendants gave rise to peoples of the ancient world (Genesis 10:22). He is listed in the genealogy of Jesus in the New Testament (Luke 3:36; *Sem*: KJV).

**Learn More:** 1 Chronicles 1:17

# SHIPHRAH

*But the midwives feared God, and did
not as the king of Egypt commanded
them, but saved the men children alive.*

EXODUS 1:17

Shiphrah and her associate, Puah, were midwives in Egypt
who assisted Israelite women during the process of
childbirth. Since they are named in the Bible, they were
probably in charge of other midwives who attended Hebrew
mothers-to-be (Exodus 1:15).

The Egyptian pharaoh was alarmed at the dramatic
increase of his Israelite slaves, particularly the males, who
could grow up to stage a revolution. So he ordered Shiphrah
and Puah to see to it that all male Israelite babies were killed
as soon as they were born (Exodus 1:15–22).

When these midwives refused to obey his command,
the king demanded an explanation. They came up with a
creative answer: these babies were born so quickly to the
strong Israelite mothers, they told him, that the midwives
could not get there in time to carry out the death order.

Foiled by the brave, clever midwives, the pharaoh then
ordered his own people to enforce his decree.

# SILAS

*And Paul chose Silas, and departed,*
*being recommended by the*
*brethren unto the grace of God.*
Acts 15:40

Silas was a believer in the early church who worked with the apostle Paul as an evangelist and church planter. The two probably first met at a gathering of church leaders in Jerusalem. This body decided that Gentiles could be saved without going through certain Jewish rituals such as circumcision.

This group sent its decision in a letter to the church at Antioch through Paul and Barnabas. Two delegates from Jerusalem, one of whom was Silas, were also appointed to go with the two missionaries. After helping deliver the good news, Silas stayed on in Antioch to help Paul and Barnabas encourage and strengthen the new believers in the city (Acts 15:22–34).

Paul enlisted Silas to accompany him on his second missionary journey. In the city of Philippi, they were beaten and imprisoned for causing a disturbance. They were praying and singing to the Lord at midnight when an earthquake shook the building, setting them free. This led to the conversion of the jailer and his family (Acts 16:25–33).

In later years, Silas apparently worked with Paul in the churches at Thessalonica (1 Thessalonians 1:1; 2 Thessalonians 1:1; *Silvanus:* KJV) and Corinth (Acts 18:5).

**Learn More:** 2 Corinthians 1:19

# SIMEON, JACOB'S SON

*And it came to pass on the third day. . .that two
of the sons of Jacob, Simeon and Levi, Dinah's
brethren, took each man his sword, and came
upon the city boldly, and slew all the males.*
GENESIS 34:25

Simeon was a son of Jacob through his wife Leah. Simeon and his full brother Levi burned with anger when a Canaanite man named Shechem violated the virginity of their sister Dinah. Pretending to invite Shechem into Jacob's family, they talked all the male inhabitants of Shechem's clan into being circumcised—the physical ritual God demanded of all males among His people. But when the Shechemites were recovering from the painful procedure, Simeon and Levi killed them all, plundered their possessions, and returned Dinah to their own camp (Genesis 34:1–29).

Later, Simeon traveled with all his brothers except Benjamin to Egypt to buy grain. Their half brother Joseph held Simeon as a hostage to make sure Joseph's younger brother Benjamin came with them when they returned (Genesis 42:23–24).

When Jacob blessed his twelve sons at the end of his life, he condemned Simeon and Levi for their act of revenge against Shechem and the other Canaanites (Genesis 49:5–7). Simeon's descendants grew into one of the twelve tribes of the nation of Israel.

**Learn More:** Genesis 34:30–31

# SIMEON, THE PROPHET

*And it was revealed unto him [Simeon] by the*
*Holy Ghost, that he should not see death,*
*before he had seen the Lord's Christ.*

LUKE 2:26

When Jesus was eight days old, Mary and Joseph brought Him to the temple in Jerusalem with an offering to present Him to the Lord. They must have been surprised when a prophet named Simeon arrived at that very moment, took the baby in his arms, and blessed the entire family.

The Holy Spirit had revealed to Simeon that he would live to see the long-awaited Messiah. Now that he had held Jesus in his arms, he was ready to die in peace (Luke 2:21–35).

But then the prophet interjected a sobering prophecy into this joyous occasion. He told Mary that this child, while He would be God's agent of redemption for many people, would cause great anguish for her. Perhaps she thought about Simeon's words more than thirty years later when she watched her firstborn Son suffer and die on the cross (John 19:25–27).

# SIMON OF CYRENE

*And as they led him away, they laid hold upon*
*one Simon, a Cyrenian, coming out of the*
*country, and on him they laid the cross,*
*that he might bear it after Jesus.*
LUKE 23:26

Simon has been immortalized as the man who carried Jesus' cross to the crucifixion site. Apparently he was just passing by when he was pressed into service for this task (Matthew 27:32).

Simon was from Cyrene, a city on the northern coast of Africa. Cyrene had a large Jewish population, so he may have been a Greek-speaking Jew who was in Jerusalem for the Passover celebration when Jesus was crucified.

Mark's gospel adds the additional detail that Simon was the father of Alexander and Rufus (Mark 15:21). This may have been the same Rufus greeted by the apostle Paul in his letter to the Christians at Rome (Romans 16:13).

After Jesus' ascension, residents of Cyrene were in Jerusalem on the day of Pentecost (Acts 2:10). Some of them became believers and were later scattered in the persecution that broke out after the martyrdom of Stephen (Acts 11:19–29).

**Learn More:** Mark 15:21

*Simon answered and said, I suppose that he,*
*to whom he forgave most. And he [Jesus]*
*said unto him, Thou hast rightly judged.*
LUKE 7:43

A Pharisee named Simon invited Jesus to his house for a meal. While they were eating, a woman who was a known sinner approached Jesus, washed His feet, and wiped them dry with her hair.

Simon was thinking that no true prophet would allow himself to be touched and contaminated by such a sinner. But Jesus read the Pharisee's thoughts and told him a brief parable to challenge his grudging attitude. If two debtors had their debts canceled, which one would love his creditor most, Jesus asked him, the person who owed little or the one who owed a much greater sum? Simon admitted that it was the person with the largest debt (Luke 7:36–47).

Jesus then drove home His point: Simon had not shown Jesus the customary hospitality extended to a guest, but this sinful woman had gone above and beyond what was expected. She had been forgiven abundantly. But Simon—a self-righteous Pharisee who thought he had no need for forgiveness—remained in his sin.

# SOLOMON

*Give therefore thy servant an understanding*
*heart to judge thy people, that I [Solomon]*
*may discern between good and bad.*
1 KINGS 3:9

As King David's successor, Solomon started well by asking God for wisdom to govern. He would complete many building projects, the most impressive being the temple in the capital city of Jerusalem (1 Kings 6:1–38).

Solomon was an effective administrator. He divided the nation into districts that funneled goods into Jerusalem to support his government. His system of trade with surrounding countries brought unprecedented wealth to Judah as well as to himself (1 Kings 9:26–28; 10:26–29).

Solomon also wrote many proverbs and other wise sayings (1 Kings 4:32). The wisdom books of Proverbs, Ecclesiastes, and Song of Solomon in the Old Testament are attributed to him, either in part or in full.

Despite his wisdom, though, Solomon's lapses in judgment are well known. He built a harem of hundreds of wives and concubines, often political unions to seal alliances with foreign nations. He allowed these women to worship their national deities and was eventually influenced by these pagan gods (1 Kings 11:1–5).

The king's expensive projects and lavish lifestyle required high taxes from his subjects. When he died, the disgruntled ten northern tribes of the nation rebelled and formed their own nation known as Israel, or the northern kingdom. The two tribes that remained loyal to Solomon and his successors continued as the nation of Judah, the southern kingdom.

**Learn More:** 1 Kings 1–3; 10:1–10 / 2 Chronicles 1–9

# STEPHEN

*And they stoned Stephen, calling upon God,*
*and saying, Lord Jesus, receive my spirit.*
ACTS 7:59

Stephen was a believer from a Greek-speaking background in the early church in Jerusalem. He, along with six other trustworthy followers of Christ, was appointed to a task force to oversee distribution of food to needy believers (Acts 6:1–7).

This zealous disciple quickly became a defender of the gospel against the Jewish religious leaders. In one of the longest speeches in the book of Acts, Stephen accused his opponents of killing Jesus the Messiah, just as their ancestors had murdered the prophets sent by the Lord in Old Testament times. He ended his remarks by declaring that he had seen a vision of God in heaven, with Jesus at His side (Acts 6:8–7:58).

Enraged, the Jewish leaders accused Stephen of blasphemy, dragged him outside the city, and stoned him to death. Watching this grisly scene was a man named Saul, one of the most passionate persecutors of the gospel (Acts 7:58–8:1). But Stephen's masterful speech and prayer for his enemies probably influenced Saul's later conversion to Christ. Saul eventually became known as the apostle Paul, world-traveling missionary to the Gentiles.

Stephen's martyrdom set off a wave of persecution that drove believers out of Jerusalem. This brought more people to the Lord as "they that were scattered abroad went every where preaching the word" (Acts 8:4).

**Learn More:** Acts 22:20

# THEOPHILUS

*It seemed good to me also, having had perfect
understanding of all things from the very first, to
write unto thee in order, most excellent Theophilus.*

LUKE 1:3

All of us are indebted to people we know very little about.
This is certainly true in the case of Theophilus, the person
for whom Luke wrote his Gospel and the book of Acts (Luke
1:1–3; Acts 1:1).

The name Theophilus means "friend of God," and this
is the only fact about him that is known for sure. Luke
could have used the name in a generic sense—that is, his
Gospel was meant for anyone who was a "friend of God."
Or, Luke's description of Theophilus as "most excellent"
could mean he was a high Roman official. Or Theophilus
could have been a novice believer who needed to be assured
of "the certainty of the things about which you have been
instructed" regarding the life and ministry of Jesus (Luke
1:4 HCSB).

No matter who he was, Theophilus was at least partially
responsible for Luke's writing of his Gospel and the book of
Acts. If not for him, many acts of Jesus and the early church
might never have been recorded and passed on to future
generations. See also *Luke.*

# THOMAS

*Jesus saith unto him, Thomas, because thou hast
seen me, thou hast believed: blessed are they
that have not seen, and yet have believed.*
JOHN 20:29

All twelve of Jesus' disciples had a hard time believing He had been raised from the dead. But Thomas was the biggest doubter of all.

Thomas was not with the rest of the group when Jesus appeared to them on the day of His resurrection. The others told Thomas they had seen Him alive, but he was not convinced. "Unless I see the nail marks in his hands and put my finger where the nails were, and put my hand into his side," he declared, "I will not believe" (John 20:25 NIV).

Eight days later, Jesus appeared again to His disciples, and personally invited Thomas to touch His wounds. This time Thomas believed and professed Jesus as his Lord and Master.

On another occasion, Jesus told the disciples He was going away to prepare a place for them. Thomas asked, "Lord, we don't know where you are going, so how can we know the way?" Jesus responded with His famous answer, "I am the way and the truth and the life. No one comes to the Father except through me" (John 14:5–6 NIV).

**Learn More:** John 11:11–16

# TIMOTHY

*For this cause have I sent unto you Timotheus,
who is my beloved son, and faithful in the
Lord, who shall bring you into remembrance
of my ways which be in Christ, as I teach
every where in every church.*
1 CORINTHIANS 4:17

During his visit to Lystra on his second missionary journey, the apostle Paul met a young believer named Timothy, or Timotheus. Impressed with his faith and commitment, the apostle invited him to join his missionary party (Acts 16:1). Timothy traveled and worked with Paul for several years, eventually becoming perhaps his most trusted and dependable missionary associate.

Timothy was apparently associated with Paul in his work at churches in several cities, including Corinth, Philippi, Colosse, and Thessalonica. Several of the apostle's letters to these congregations—as well as his epistle to Philemon—open with greetings from Paul as well as Timothy.

Paul's important work in Ephesus also had a Timothy connection. After the apostle worked in this city for more than two years, he apparently left Timothy in charge and moved on to plant churches in other locations (1 Timothy 1:3).

Paul addressed two of his pastoral epistles to Timothy as a church leader. The apostle encouraged his associate to act with integrity in spite of his young age (1 Timothy 4:12) and to base his actions on the teachings of the Bible.

**Learn More:** Acts 17:5; 19:22 / Philippians 2:19

# TITUS

*Nevertheless God, that comforteth
those that are cast down,
comforted us by the coming of Titus.*
2 Corinthians 7:6

An associate of the apostle Paul, Titus performed several important tasks in the churches founded by the apostle. Titus carried letters from Paul to the troubled church at Corinth and reported back to the apostle on how the congregation was dealing with these problems (2 Corinthians 2:13; 7:5–16).

This dependable missionary appears in another important role in the church on the island of Crete. Paul sent him there to deal with false teachings and to strengthen the new believers in their faith. The apostle addressed one of his pastoral epistles to Titus, encouraging him to teach sound doctrine (Titus 2:1) and to appoint elders to lead the church (Titus 1:5–9).

Titus was also associated with evangelistic work in the province of Dalmatia (2 Timothy 4:10). Paul referred to him as "mine own son after the common faith" (Titus 1:4).

**Learn More:** Galatians 2:1–3

# URIAH

*But Uriah slept at the door of the king's house with all the servants of his lord, and went not down to his house.*

2 Samuel 11:9

Uriah was a brave warrior whose death was arranged by King David to cover up his adulterous relationship with Uriah's wife, Bathsheba. How it all came about shows a serious abuse of power by one of the Bible's most admirable characters.

The affair occurred while Uriah was away from Jerusalem on a military campaign. When Bathsheba got pregnant, the king had Uriah sent home on leave so he would sleep with his wife and thus make it seem that the unborn child had been fathered by her soldier husband.

But Uriah refused to enjoy himself at home while his fellow soldiers were on the battlefield. So David got Uriah drunk in a desperate attempt to get him to change his mind. But still the soldier refused.

Finally, David sent Uriah back to the front lines. He didn't realize he was carrying his own death sentence—a letter from the king to his commander to station Uriah in the thick of battle with limited support (2 Samuel 11:14–17).

This plot succeeded, and Uriah was killed. David waited until Bathsheba's period of mourning for her husband was over. Then he brought her to the royal palace as one of his wives (2 Samuel 11:26–27).

**Learn More:** 2 Samuel 23:8–39

# UZZA

*And the anger of the LORD was kindled against*
*Uzza, and he smote him, because he put his*
*hand to the ark: and there he died before God.*
1 CHRONICLES 13:10

Shortly after David was made king of all Israel, he decided to restore the nearly-forgotten ark of the covenant to its proper prominence. So he ordered men, including Uzza, to bring it from Kirjath-Jearim to Jerusalem. These men were not Levites, the tribe assigned to such holy duties, and they unwisely put the ark on an oxcart rather than carrying it on poles as God had instructed Moses.

When the oxen stumbled, Uzza reached out to steady the ark, and was immediately struck dead for "his error" (2 Samuel 6:7). The incident frightened David, who asked himself, "How shall I bring the ark of God home to me?" (1 Chronicles 13:12). Three months later, though, having set up a tent for the ark in Jerusalem, David tried again, this time calling on the Levites and demanding that they follow God's instructions to the letter.

**Learn More:** 2 Samuel 6:1–11 / 1 Chronicles 13

# UZZIAH

*He [Uzziah]. . .transgressed against the L<small>ORD</small> his
God, and went into the temple of the L<small>ORD</small> to
burn incense upon the altar of incense.*
2 C<small>HRONICLES</small> 26:16

King Uzziah of Judah—also known as Azariah and Ozias—
obeyed God and governed wisely during a time of great
prosperity for his country. A good military strategist, he
defeated the Philistines and the Ammonites, fortified key
cities, and built up his army to protect Judah from enemy
attacks.

The king also improved living conditions for his people by
digging wells to provide water for their crops and livestock.
His progressive policies were admired by the surrounding
peoples of the region (2 Chronicles 26:1–15).

But Uzziah's success brought out his dark side. Proud of
his achievements, he decided to try his hand at offering a
sacrifice in the temple—a role reserved for priests. When he
prepared to burn incense, the priests stopped him. He lashed
out in anger, and was struck with leprosy that sidelined him
for the rest of his life (2 Chronicles 26:16–21).

Uzziah's reign of fifty-two years was one of the longest
in Judah's history. Isaiah was called to the prophetic ministry
through a stirring vision of God "in the year that King Uzziah
died" (Isaiah 6:1).

**Learn More:** 2 Kings 15:1–7; *Azariah:* KJV / Amos 1:1 /
Matthew 1:8–10; *Ozias:* KJV

# ZACCHAEUS

*And he [Zacchaeus] ran before, and climbed
up into a sycomore tree to see him [Jesus]:
for he was to pass that way.*

Luke 19:4

As a chief tax collector, Zacchaeus probably had other agents for the Roman government working under his supervision. This coveted position in the city of Jericho had made him a rich man.

Zacchaeus was anxious to get a glimpse of Jesus as He passed through Jericho on His way to Jerusalem. Since Zacchaeus was not very tall, he climbed a tree to get a better view. The tax collector must have been shocked when Jesus called him down. Then Jesus invited Himself to Zacchaeus's house for a visit (Luke 19:1–10)!

As he talked with Jesus, Zacchaeus faced up to some of the less-than-ethical things he had done in his profession. He promised to repay the people he had cheated four times more than what he had taken. He also vowed to give half of what he owned to the poor.

Jesus welcomed Zacchaeus into God's kingdom and added that "he also is a son of Abraham" (verse 9). The Jewish people hated tax collectors. But Jesus declared that Zacchaeus's profession had nothing to do with his status as a Jewish citizen. Even a despised agent of the Roman government could respond to the grace of God.

# ZACHARIAS

*And Zacharias said unto the angel,*
*Whereby shall I know this? for I am an old*
*man, and my wife well stricken in years.*
LUKE 1:18

The priest Zacharias and his wife, Elisabeth, had not been able to have children. And the possibility of that happening was slim, since both were in their senior years.

But God had other plans for this good couple. While Zacharias was going about his priestly duties in the temple, an angel told him that Elisabeth would give birth to a son. They should call him John, a name meaning "God has been gracious." This miracle child would become God's special messenger who would "make ready a people prepared for the Lord" (Luke 1:17; see 1:5–25).

Because Zacharias expressed doubt that this would happen, the angel took away his ability to speak. Imagine what anguish he must have felt at not being able to tell others that he was going to be a father in his old age.

After John was born, the speech of Zacharias returned. In a beautiful song known as the Benedictus, he praised the Lord for sending this son who would prepare the way for the coming Messiah. His son grew up to become John the Baptist, forerunner of Jesus the Messiah (Luke 1:67–80). See also *Elisabeth*.

**Learn More:** Luke 1:57–64

# ZECHARIAH

*In the eighth month, in the second year*
*of Darius, came the word of the LORD*
*unto Zechariah, the son of Berechiah,*
*the son of Iddo the prophet.*

ZECHARIAH 1:1

The prophet Zechariah delivered his messages to the people of Judah during the years after they returned from exile. Perhaps the most famous passage from his book is his prediction that the future Messiah would enter the city of Jerusalem "riding on a donkey, on a colt, the foal of a donkey" (Zechariah 9:9 HCSB). Matthew quoted this verse in his Gospel to show that Jesus fulfilled Zechariah's prophecy in His triumphal entry into the Holy City (Matthew 21:5).

Zechariah is also known for his symbolic language about the end times—a literary form similar to the visions in the books of Daniel and Revelation. In one of Zechariah's visions, God appeared as a lampstand beside two olive trees. These trees symbolized Zerubbabel and Joshua, two people whom God had charged with the task of rebuilding the temple in Jerusalem (Zechariah 4:1–14).

Zechariah ministered in Judah at about the same time as the priest Ezra. Zechariah's prophecies occur in the Old Testament book that bears his name.

**Learn More:** Ezra 5:1; 6:14

# ZELOPHEHAD

*And the Lord spake unto Moses, saying,*
*The daughters of Zelophehad speak right:*
*thou shalt surely give them a possession*
*of an inheritance among their father's*
*brethren; and thou shalt cause the*
*inheritance of their father to pass unto them.*

NUMBERS 27:6–7

Zelophehad, a member of the tribe of Manasseh, died in the wilderness during the exodus from Egypt. He had no sons who would inherit his property after he settled in Canaan. But he did have five intelligent and far-sighted daughters—Mahlah, Noah, Hoglah, Milcah, and Tirzah.

These daughters approached Moses with a request: they wanted to inherit their father's property in the distribution of land that was coming to him when the people entered Canaan. Moses agreed, but he made it clear that each of them must marry within their father's tribe. This would assure that the land allotted to each of the twelve tribes would always be owned by members of the tribal group to which it was first granted (Numbers 36:7; see 27:1–7).

Their request was granted years later when the Israelites conquered Canaan and settled on the land (Joshua 17:3–6).

**Learn More:** Numbers 26:33

# ZERUBBABEL

*The hands of Zerubbabel have laid the*
*foundation of this house; his hands shall*
*also finish it; and thou shalt know that the*
*Lord of hosts hath sent me unto you.*
ZECHARIAH 4:9

Zerubbabel faced a difficult task—rebuilding the temple in Jerusalem after the Jewish exiles returned to their homeland (Ezra 1:1–3; 2:1–2). This building had been in ruins for several decades since its destruction by the Babylonians. Enemies of the Jews opposed the rebuilding effort and even succeeded in getting it stopped for several years (Ezra 4:1–24). The Jewish people themselves waxed hot and cold in their commitment to the project.

With prodding from two Old Testament prophets (Haggai 2:1–3; Zechariah 4:6–10), Zerubbabel finally completed the task. It was dedicated with great fanfare, but mysteriously Zerubbabel is not mentioned in connection with the celebration (Ezra 6:14–22).

This building—often referred to as "Zerubbabel's Temple"—was not as ornate as the original structure built by King Solomon several centuries before. The exiles who returned to Judah sometimes used this as an excuse for not working diligently on the project. But the prophet Haggai kept the pressure on with these encouraging words: "'The final glory of this house will be greater than the first,' says the Lord of Hosts. 'I will provide peace in this place'—this is the declaration of the Lord of Hosts" (Haggai 2:9 HCSB).

**Learn More:** Ezra 3:8; 5:2

# ALSO FROM GEORGE W. KNIGHT

## The No-Stress Bible Guide

You want to study the Bible, but it's easy to be discouraged by the ponderous guides and tedious systematic reading plans on the market. *The No-Stress Bible Guide* addresses these shortcomings by combining a flexible reading plan with easy-to-understand notes on major sections of God's Word. Plus, it's beautifully illustrated in color!

Paperback / 978-1-64352-018-6 / $16.99